Kingdom and Empire

"Tempelmeyer's imagination, for the church, brings about both shame and hope. His revelation of what the church has become, matched with the challenge to strive for an imaginative faith, should motivate every Christian to examine every nook and cranny of their lives and step forward on a journey of change. All this for the hope of the church and for the cause of Christ, the one we ought to know. He's right: 'what the church believes is real.' My feelings and questions have both been evoked."

—TIM MCCOY
Executive Minister, Canadian Baptists of Ontario and Quebec

Kingdom and Empire

Seeking God's Kingdom from within
the World's Wealthiest Nations

GENE TEMPELMEYER

RESOURCE *Publications* · Eugene, Oregon

KINGDOM AND EMPIRE
Seeking God's Kingdom from within the World's Wealthiest Nations

Resource Publications
An Imprint of Wipf and Stock Publishers
199 W. 8th Ave., Suite 3
Eugene, OR 97401

www.wipfandstock.com

PAPERBACK ISBN: 978-1-6667-1628-3
HARDCOVER ISBN: 978-1-6667-1629-0
EBOOK ISBN: 978-1-6667-1630-6

08/31/21

Contents

Acknowledgments

THERE ARE MANY FINGERPRINTS on this book. The people of Spring Garden Church, Toronto, helped hone the ideas. Debbie Tempelmeyer and Jeff Crosby pushed me to push this project to a published conclusion. Claire Brubaker brought expertise and insight as editor. Wipf and Stock took a chance on an unknown writer. I am grateful to you all.

Introduction

IT'S A GOOD NIGHT for a movie. We'll go to the theater, be in our seats in time for the previews, and fill ourselves with popcorn drenched in the hydrogenated oil product they call "melted butter."

The story line of the film we're about to see involves an empire and a small band of rebels trying to live independently despite the overwhelming power and influence of the empire. How do you expect the story and characters to unfold?

Wherever or whenever the film is set, what values do you expect the empire to hold and express? Who are the good guys? Are they the people wearing the empire's uniform and keeping the peace? Or are the good guys the rebels dedicated to breaking the empire's power over their lives and families?

I don't know about you, but I expect the empire to possess walls, weapons, and wealth. Whether the story is set in the past, present, or some dystopian future, I predict the empire will use its walls, weapons, and wealth to generate constant expansion. It will never be enough. The empire will continue amassing more wealth, territory, peoples, and power until the empire's reach causes the center to implode. Or those pesky rebels win.

What motivates the empire to pursue this constant expansion is the conviction that this is the only way they can fully protect and provide for those within the empire.

Much of the Bible is set in the context of empires. The narrative of the children of Israel is largely about how the people of God relate to empires around and over them. Through almost all the Bible the direction of this relationship is God's people either under threat or under the thumb of one empire or another: Egypt, Assyria, Babylon, Persia, or Rome.

The question God's people must ask in this situation is: How do we live within the kingdom of God (and how does the kingdom of God live within us!) while there is an army pointing its guns at us and declaring, "Like it or not, you serve the empire. If you can serve your God while you serve the empire, well enough! But you *will* serve the empire!"

Remember the first time you saw Star Wars? Luke Skywalker was in his cool fighter spaceship flying through a valley on the surface of the Death Star. He pushed the flight assists out of the way, trusted the force, fired his weapon, hit the target, and ran for cover as the Death Star exploded in a huge conflagration.

How did you feel the first time you saw that? *Yes!!!* He got them! Way to go, Luke!

But how would you feel if you lived in the Death Star? It was under construction. What if your parents were there as engineers on the project? What if your sister or brother were an imperial trooper? How would you feel about Luke Skywalker, Han Solo, or Princess Leia if you had grown up in the empire and it was your home?

I live in a suburban house on the outskirts of Toronto in Canada. I grew up in the southern United States. I am from the empire. Chances are good that you are, too. We live in the part of the world where people want to build walls to protect our affluence from people who would like to live with some of the wealth and benefits we enjoy. Our empire may be more economic than military or political. Wealth and power, nevertheless, travel together.

I didn't choose to live in the empire, and I don't feel guilty about it. It just is what it is. But it is never a bad idea to recognize reality. In the terms of the biblical narrative: I'm Egyptian. I'm Roman.

I'm a nice person. I'm caring. I'm compassionate. Just as I am sure there were nice, caring, and compassionate people in Babylon. Those nice, caring, compassionate Babylonians likely saw things through the lens of being at home in Babylon. From this perspective the conquest of Judah would not have seemed such a horrible thing. In fact, it was probably good for the Israelites to be introduced to the greatest civilization in the world! It's all a matter of perspective. A standpoint is simply the limited view we see from where we happen to be standing.

If a great deal of the Bible is about conflict between empires and the people who belong to God, how does living in the empire change the way we read the Bible? If I lived on the Death Star and watched a film critical of the Roman Empire, I doubt I would recognize my own context of empire. If I thought this was a sacred story describing the work and will of God, there are a lot of things in the story I would probably not pay attention to, or would spiritualize away. I might think Rome simply served as a metaphor for the sins and moral indiscretions of individual people. It's unlikely I would think God really wanted to destroy my way of life.

When we read the Bible from inside the empire, there is much we unconsciously overlook. This is the only way we can resolve cognitive dissonance, the inner tension when we think conflicting thoughts. We are likely to enjoy and celebrate those parts of the Bible that support our values and challenge us to live better personal lives in the empire. But we are not likely to notice or mark the ways the Bible critiques our use of walls, weapons, and wealth.

Most followers of Jesus genuinely and sincerely want to live for the kingdom of God in the world. Living in the Western world, we will not be able to live fully for the kingdom until we realize we actually are part of the empire.

It will take discipline and awareness to read the Bible faithfully so that we don't miss its critique of the empire. We will need to beware the constant temptation to rationalize or spiritualize away the warnings issued to the empire by prophets, apostles, and Jesus.

God is not necessarily asking us to leave the empire. When the Jewish people found themselves living in the heart of the empire, Jeremiah had these words for them:

> Build houses and live in them; plant gardens and eat
> their produce. Take wives and have sons and daughters;

take wives for your sons, and give your daughters in marriage, that they may bear sons and daughters; multiply
there, and do not decrease. But seek the welfare of the
city where I have sent you into exile, and pray to the Lord
on its behalf, for in its welfare you will find your welfare.
(Jeremiah 29:5–7)

As people who live for the kingdom, we have to think seriously about the welfare of the city in which we find ourselves.
How would King Jesus understand the welfare of the place we live?
Would he see that welfare enhanced by more walls, more wealth,
and more weapons? Or would he ask us to live in such a way that
the empire might be redeemed?

After all, God loves Egyptians. He loves Babylonians, Romans, and Death Star storm troopers, too. But the values of the
empire make it hard to fully understand and embrace God's love
and mercy. Such love and mercy cannot be comprehended apart
from extending love and mercy to all God's creation. Empires are
not good at that.

A rich young ruler once came to Jesus looking for the key
to an infinitely full and rich life. Jesus replied that to find such a
life, this rich ruler would have to make what he had available to
people without as much. The young ruler went away in sorrow. After all, what good is it being a rich ruler if you have to give up your
wealth and power? Following Jesus is a lot more attractive when
it doesn't require us to share with people who haven't "earned for
themselves" as much as we have.

Yet, the God revealed in Christ is a God who emptied himself, who gave up power and wealth in exchange for birth in a
stable, a sparse lifestyle, and death by a means the empire reserved
exclusively for slaves and insurgents.

The apostle Paul was a citizen of the empire. He found a way
to use that citizenship for the kingdom of God. He used the empire's roads and infrastructure to spread the message that Jesus is
Lord, not Caesar. Of course, the empire executed him, too. But for
Paul, living the values of the kingdom meant even his death was
considered a gain. He served a higher cause than his own comfort,

wealth, and security. In other words, he could remain a citizen of the empire, but he did not have to live by its values. He was in the empire, but the empire was not in him.

This book is about living for the kingdom of God from the middle of the empire. The first step may be simply recognizing that we are citizens of the empire. This makes us different from the vast majority of people we meet in the Bible. Israel and the earliest church were not part of their dominant empires. In fact, they were subjugated by the empire. They were the conquered and enslaved.

We are in an unusual position. We enjoy the benefits of the empire. We have material resources and personal freedom well beyond what most of the people who inhabit the Bible possessed. But is this an opportunity for us? Or is it, perhaps, a temptation?

1

The First Empire

ABOUT THE TIME I started school, my grandmother gave me a book of illustrated Bible stories. I don't remember many of the pictures, but I do remember them colorfully sparking my imagination. The picture I remember best is one that puzzled me.

It was a painting of workers building something out of brick that looked like a flat-bottomed ice-cream cone turned upside down. Construction scaffolding reached almost to the clouds.

"What's this?"

"The Tower of Babel. That's where God gave people all the different languages around the world."

"Why?"

"They were trying to build this tower so high they could climb into heaven. So, God mixed up their words. Then no one could understand what they were saying to each other and they couldn't finish building the tower."

I did not have a theological education, so this did not make sense at all. Frankly, several decades of study and a couple of theological degrees later, it still makes no sense. Even at five or six years old I knew that no one could build a tower high enough to poke through the sky and reach God. I explained this to my grandmother.

The adults in the room had to agree I was correct. You can't build a tower to heaven.

"So why did God have to stop them?"

If there was an answer to that question, I don't recall it. I do recall seeing that picture whenever I leafed through the book and wondering every time I saw it what it really was.

That infamous tower is where we can best begin exploring the theme of empire in the Bible. If you live in the empire, its easiest to assume this is simply a story about the origins of diverse human language and all the implications of that diversity. Looking a little more deeply, however, this story calls into question some of the values most of us build our lives on. Values that are often incorporated into our religious beliefs.

So, let's look a little more carefully. "And as people migrated from the east, they found a plain in the land of Shinar and settled there. And they said to one another, 'Come, let us make bricks and burn them thoroughly.' And they had brick for stone and bitumen for mortar" (Genesis 11:2–3).

The devil, as they say, is in the details. The significance of this location is identified in the previous chapter. There we meet one of the most historically significant, yet largely unknown, characters of the Bible. His name was Nimrod. His significance is described in only five verses. Here is what we learn in that brief summary about Nimrod:

- He was "the first on earth to be a mighty man."
- He is also described as "a mighty hunter."
- He became a king in the land of Shinar, where he ruled over four communities.
- During his reign he expanded his kingdom to include several other territories and a "great city."

The Hebrew word translated "mighty" implies fighting ability. This would have made Nimrod an effective hunter. What was his prey? Cities, land, and people. When a person begins with a base of people, power, and land and uses their strength to prey upon and accumulate more people, power, and land, what do we call it? In our society, we call that a great success! But we also call it an empire. Nimrod is the first emperor.

The base from which Nimrod's empire began to expand was the land of Shinar, where people built a famous tower.

It was a new kind of tower when they began construction. Someone had developed an innovative construction technology. Two technologies, actually. They had learned how to make their own stone out of brick. Prior to this, building with stones was inefficient and time consuming. As stones are found in nature, they are hard to stack high because of their irregular shapes. To cut stones into shapes that are easily stackable is a labor- and time-intensive process. But if you can manufacture flat-sided, uniform bricks, you can stack a lot of them in a fraction of the time.

Add together the adhesive quality of bitumen tar and the flat, uniform shape that bricks offer, and not only can permanent structures be built quickly, but they can be built stronger and higher. Because they can be shaped so regularly, that strength comes in a more compact form.

New technologies don't just change how we do things. They change how we live, and in changing how we live, they change how we think about and understand life and our place in the world. The new technology developed on the plains in Shinar made a new kind of community possible. The ability to construct permanent dwellings in a compact space and then surround those dwellings with a strong wall drew people together in more concentrated communities. Though they were very much smaller than today's urban landscapes, we call these concentrated communities *cities*.

High walls, in turn, created a new way of thinking about people. There are those inside our wall and those outside our wall. Insiders and outsiders. Us and them.

Technology has made life much easier in many ways. Every evening after supper, I am grateful to whomever invented the dishwasher. I keep discovering things such as heated car seats and streaming music. I never knew how much I needed these things until I used them. I don't know how I ever communicated to a crowd before PowerPoint or studied before colored highlighters!

We don't always see the long-term implications of new technology. I remember standing at the sink singing with my mother when it was my turn to wash or dry dishes. I realize I have exchanged ease for something more valuable. But I'm not getting rid of my dishwasher, nevertheless. Toothpaste is not the only new technology that can't be squeezed back into the tube.

This is the challenge of technology. We have the technological capacity to do amazing things. But we haven't developed a corresponding moral capacity to know whether we actually *should* do them.

The new technology of bricks and bitumen came, as new technologies so often do, with unintended consequences.

> And the Lord said, "Behold, they are one people, and they have one language, and this is only the beginning of what they will do. And nothing that they propose to do will now be impossible for them. Come, let us go down and confuse their language so that they may not understand one another's speech." (Genesis 11:6–7)

If we are to accurately understand the Bible, it is necessary to understand the thought of the people inspired by God to write and to understand how they thought their words would be read by their contemporaries. With regard to this story, we should remember ancient Hebrews saw God as the ultimate cause of everything that happens. When they wrote about God generating a multitude of languages, they were describing a cause. It is not necessarily a punishment, but simply a direct and natural response to the development.

Rather than punishing children by imposing a consequence that has nothing to do with the behavior a parent wants to modify, I think it is a far more effective strategy to let children suffer some of the natural consequences of their poor decisions. For example, telling a child they will lose dessert tonight if they run out into the street is not as effective as telling them they will have to walk along holding Mother's hand if they can't be trusted to stay with her. Holding Mom's hand is a natural outcome of leaving her side.

A confusing multitude of languages is not a punishment for building a tower. It is, however, a natural consequence.

Here's how it works: if we create a technology that separates us into distinct groups of people, we will begin to think and behave like distinct groups of people. If Nimrod is going to expand his empire by powerfully preying upon people and communities, and if he has a technology that seems to make him invincible, it is only a matter of time before those threatened communities begin to copy his technology and develop their own. We will create our own unique cultures and identities to help define ourselves as distinct from "you" and "them." And, truly, it is hard to understand people who have developed a different culture from our own, much as we may genuinely want to be open and understanding.

Wherever one group of people decides they can best protect themselves and prosper by preying upon others, it is a natural consequence that those others will band together to create their own competing empire. As new technology breeds new wealth and ability, power shifts to where technology and wealth can be most efficiently put to use. Every empire that rises eventually falls to some upstart who figured out how to make bricks and stick them together.

Another interpretive insight we should bring to this story is the nature of the first eleven chapters of Genesis. These chapters carry us from creation, through losing the garden, Cain and Abel, the flood, and, finally, to the Tower of Babel. The story of the tower is a pivot point at which Genesis shifts from one kind of literature to another.

The first eleven chapters of Genesis form a prehistory. They are a collection of oral traditions passed down from generation to generation. The truth of these stories is not the details of the events they describe but what they suggest about who we are.

I don't think it is necessary, but if you read these stories as literal history, that's okay with me. It does no harm *so long as* you don't get so caught up in defending the literal accuracy of the details you ignore their actual meaning in the world this year. (And so long as you don't turn this conviction into another way of separating us from them. Religion is not immune to the thought processes of empire.)

These early stories tell us who we are. What these stories tell us about ourselves is completely accurate. *Genesis* literally means "origins," and this part of the Bible is given to reveal fundamental truths about how humans act and experience.

Nimrod's history is not nearly as important as recognizing the continuing presence of Nimrod today. The Tower of Babel falls under the category of "current events." *Rich Christians in an Age of Hunger*, by Ronald Sider, was first published in 1977.[1] In this prescient book, Sider warns that as a minority of the world's population becomes more and more wealthy while the majority becomes more and more impoverished, it is only a matter of time before people of the Majority World begin crashing the wealthy minority's party.

As I write, several Nimrods around the Minority World are busy figuring out how to use bricks and bitumen to keep the impoverished majority at a safe distance. "We" have walls and weapons to protect our wealth from "them." At least in my part of the empire, we forget that "we" came from somewhere else, too, and stole this land from a different "them," who now live in poverty. No wonder some of us fear replacement! We have seen firsthand what replacement looks like.

Nimrod is definitely not dead.

This is not to say that the Tower of Babel is a political story rather than a religious story. There are many who have suggested that the tower was an astrological platform in the service of ancient Near Eastern religion. It has also been suggested that the tower was, in fact, the first pagan shrine, the first idolatrous temple.

We don't really know with certainty how the tower was meant to be used. But it would deny history to suggest religious people don't build divisive empires. In fact, empires may even need religion. But they also need to control it.

---

1. Sider, *Rich Christians in an Age of Hunger*.

Think of this genesis of human behavior. People who have lived as nomads are gathering together into compact communities such as they had never experienced. How can life be managed in community when people have been making their own decisions and determining their own patterns? How helpful would it be to the governance of these communities to have a strong set of shared beliefs and rituals? In fact, what if we could add to those beliefs and rituals a tribal deity who would reward those who conform to the values the community wants to promote and punish those who don't? Even better, what if this deity belongs only to "us"? This deity is "our" god and no one else's! Isn't religion useful to Nimrod?!

But only if Nimrod controls the deity and its prophets and priests. If Nimrod confers wealth and power to these shamans, they will hold tightly to their symbiotic relationship with the empire. So, empires build beautiful cathedrals and towers. But remember the law of unintended consequences. These massive religious shrines become, in fact, prisons for the tribal deity. The money and glory given to its shamans guarantee their allegiance to Nimrod.

The outcome of the Tower of Babel has reached a tipping point in the last century. Nimrod builds a wall. So, a new emperor develops a technology to attack the wall by throwing stones at it. Yet another empire develops arrows so the stone-throwing machine can't get too close. Then an empire invents a cannon. And so it goes until an empire invents nuclear capacity to vaporize the whole world.

The human race has reached a point where it makes no sense to continue to expand our destructive capacity. The race to protect ourselves from each other has placed us in the greatest peril humanity has ever faced. How's that for irony?

How do we live for the kingdom of God in the midst of such competing empires?

The conflict of kingdom and empire is only a subplot to the main narrative of the Bible. The prehistory in the first eleven chapters of Genesis simply sets the stage for the main plot to emerge. That prehistory begins with a "good" creation and a "very good" humanity. But, always wanting to be like God, humanity becomes increasing violent. First come Cain and Abel. Then the destruction of the flood because the world had become full of violence. And now, on the plains of Shinar, violence goes beyond the personal and into the corporate agenda of competing empires.

The name Nimrod means "rebel." In Nimrod the broken harmony of creation reaches new levels of institutionalized division. Another way of saying this is: in Nimrod sin reaches a new level of structured divisions. The salvation of humanity—indeed, the salvation of all creation—requires a rejection of Nimrod. The world needs an alternative to competing empires and the mode of thinking that creates empires in the first place. It is an imperial mode of thinking that breaks our harmony not only with each other on all kinds of personal levels, but also among families, tribes, and nations, with nature, and with God.

In Genesis 12 God will begin to restore the universe to its lost harmony. He will start with a man named Abraham. In a world of tribes and nationalities, of us and them, God promises that he will birth from Abraham a new nation.

We might say to that proposal, "Does the world really need another nation? Another tribe? Another competing language and culture?" If this new nation were to be like the other nations divided at Babel, then certainly not.

But the nation God promised to birth through Abraham was to be different from all the other nations and peoples. This fundamental difference has too often been forgotten and lost, not least by those who consider themselves one way or another to be children of Abraham.

The new nation God wished to create in response to the division of Babel was to be a nation "through whom all the families of the earth shall be blessed" (Genesis 12:3). Rather than an empire that would conquer the world, God wanted to create through Abraham an alternative sort of nation that would see its fundamental reason for existence as blessing every nation on earth.

It is worth noting that Abraham's origins are identified as in Ur of the Chaldeans. Part of the Mesopotamian Empire, Ur was located in the region of Shinar: the land where Nimrod began an empire, people tried to build a tower, and humans became divided by language, culture, and an inability to understand each other.

Could this be coincidence? Or could it be that the narrative is designed to highlight how God drew Abraham out of the Mesopotamian Empire to launch from empire's ground zero a meaningful alternative to empire?

While Nimrod and his fellows perpetually forced other nations into the service of their empires, God offered the children of Abraham the possibility of being a people who would define themselves by serving the nations of the world. Empire is a collective expression of human sin and violence. It is rooted in the idolatrous effort to be God's equal. It is idolatrous, because God's nature is to love. Empire can only serve a false god. Serving the true God, who simply gives himself to humanity, would require an empire to stop being an empire.

So let's see how this story and this nation work out.

2

Positive Imagination

EVERYONE HAS AN ACTIVE imagination. But not everyone realizes they have an active imagination. When a person bemoans their lack of imagination, I like to ask what goes through their mind in the early hours of the morning when they lie awake worrying.

"Oh, my! Then I have an imagination! My mind runs away with all the dire things that could go wrong."

"You see," I say, "You don't lack imagination. In fact, you clearly have a vivid imagination. It's just that you are imagining the wrong things. What if you could replace your negative imagination with a more positive imagination? What if, instead of imagining in great detail what it would look like for everything to go wrong, you imagined what it could look like if everything were right?"

This can be achieved with some mental discipline and careful monitoring of our internal dialogue.

I was lying on our family-room floor in Tennessee watching a little black-and-white television when I first heard a speech in 1963. I was not old enough to nearly begin to understand the context or meaning of this speech. But I knew, perhaps if only by how it moved my parents, that I had just heard something of great importance.

A Baptist preacher was describing his dream of what my southern world might become. At the time, I lived in a town with schools for white children and one rundown school for black children. The town operated one swimming pool for white citizens and, tucked into the black corner of town, another swimming pool for black citizens. So it went.

On our little television a black preacher in Washington, DC, was imagining a different kind of world: a dream that would not only reshape his world but mine as well. He imagined little white boys like me playing with little black kids like his children. He imagined descendants of plantation owners sitting at the family table sharing a cool glass of iced tea and mutual friendship with the descendants of slaves. He imagined southern politicians replacing white supremacy with human equality, freedom, and justice for all races of people. What a beautiful, crazy dream of the end of racism in America!

The foundation of his imagination was the words of an Old Testament prophet.

> Every valley shall be lifted up,
> and every mountain and hill be made low;
> the uneven ground shall become level,
> and the rough places a plain.
> And the glory of the Lord shall be revealed,
> and all flesh shall see it together,
> for the mouth of the Lord has spoken. (Isaiah 40:4–5)

Dr. Martin Luther King Jr.'s "I Have a Dream" speech is not only an excellent example of positive imagination; it is an equally excellent example of what Walter Brueggemann calls "prophetic imagination" in an excellent book with this title.[1]

It is hard enough to imagine what incremental improvements might look like. ("What if we added a third blade to the razor?") Dr. King was imagining something far beyond incremental improvement. He was imagining a different kind of world. He was imagining a society unlike any society that has ever existed, unlike

---

1. Brueggemann, *Prophetic Imagination*.

anything that he or anyone else had ever experienced. This is prophetic imagination: imagining what it could be like if God really stepped into all the details.

Moses provides us with another excellent example of prophetic imagination. In the previous chapter we considered the empire that began on the plains of Shinar, where a tower was being constructed utilizing new technologies. Nimrod's empire leveraged that technology into economic and military dominance over his corner of the world.

In this chapter we move ahead one book in the Bible to another empire. The biblical narrative has been following the story of Abraham, through whom God promised to create a new nation that would bless all peoples on earth: every ethnicity, tribe, language, and nation. God had a global mission for the children of Abraham.

But by the time of Moses and the start of the book of Exodus, the children of Abraham were not in a position to have any kind of global influence. They were slaves in Egypt. Exodus 5 identifies the specific task the children of Abraham were performing for their Egyptian masters. They were making bricks for the empire's construction projects.

Wait a minute! Wasn't that the new technology being used in Babel? This is one of those details that makes me realize the Bible does not consist of a lot of random events, but of themes and motifs that run from one text to another. If we miss these recurring themes, we miss much of the meaning.

The children of Abraham had become slaves using a technology from which they would not themselves benefit. They were giving their lives for someone else's empire. As empires love to do, the Egyptians were building monuments to their own supremacy and exploiting the labor of those they had dominated to do so. But God heard the groans of the slaves.

Military, political, and economic dominance run together. This is how empires operate. When I consider the plight of the enslaved children of Israel giving their lives for someone else's benefit, I begin to wonder how it feels to work in a clothing factory in

Pakistan or China. In many parts of the world today people are laboring in dangerous and unjust conditions manufacturing things for me that the people doing the actual work could never afford to buy. Unless, that is, these things eventually get shipped back as secondhand goods after I have finished with them.

We all know this is the case. Yet we are, for the most part, inured to it. And it is complicated in that, if we don't buy those cheap products, it may deprive these same workers of what little employment they have. The problem is systemic. We can't change it unless we can imagine a world that is completely different from the world as we have been experiencing it.

An interesting word appeared in several ancient Near Eastern dialects in about 2000 BC. *Habiru* described a group of people not defined by race, tribe, or any other sort of national identity. They came from many places but owned none of them. They were nationless people who lived on the margins of whatever society they could. They often found themselves hired out as mercenaries or pressed into slavery because, with no land or wealth base of their own, these were the only ways they could survive.

Habiru means "dusty and dirty." It is the *habiru* today who get on small boats in North Africa and hope they reach Europe before the boat capsizes. They collect at border crossings in Mexico and Calais prepared to risk everything because they have so little to lose.

Because the word *habiru* began to appear at about the time of Moses, it is sometimes supposed that it is simply another form of the word *Hebrew*. This is not the case. The etymological roots of these words are different. Again, the *habiru* came from many tribes and languages.

The word *Hebrew* was first used by Abraham's neighbors to describe Abraham and his family. Literally, it means "from the other side." Abraham's family origins are in Ur of the Chaldeans, which was on the other side of the Euphrates River from Canaan, where Abraham eventually settled.

But the designation "from the other side" described more than the geography of a river. Abraham was from the dominant empire east of the Canaanites. Like all nearby empires, Abraham's people were a threatening presence. Abraham and Lot came from the empire with a great deal of wealth, which was measured in livestock. This consumed significant resources in the Canaanite countryside. We detect from incidents recorded in Genesis that Canaanites tended to regard Abraham and Lot in much the same way too many evangelical Christians regard Muslim immigrants who show up in North America with their Islamic culture intact. "Those people are from the other side."

The children of Abraham in Egypt were both *Hebrew*, from the other side, and *habiru*, dusty and dirty. Landless, poor, and enslaved, these people seemed poor material from which to start a great nation in the middle of several very powerful empires.

Moses found himself uniquely equipped to step into this situation. He was born Hebrew. But, seeing the growing number of people from the other side in the population of the empire, Pharaoh made the decision to kill all Hebrew boys. He was concerned that the Egyptians themselves would be replaced by Hebrews otherwise.

Of course, Egyptians were willing to have a small number of people from the other side. "We'd be happy to take a few of these dirty, dusty people to do some of the miserable jobs no self-respecting Egyptian actually wants. But if too many of them come, they'll take over." Sadly, this ancient way of thinking did not die out long ago.

Rather than submit her son to Egyptian swords, Moses' mother set him afloat in a basket on a river. Discovered by Pharaoh's daughter, Moses was not only rescued but adopted into the house of the emperor. He grew right in the very heart of the empire.

No matter who adopted him, Moses would always be a Hebrew. He would always be from the other side of the tracks. No one around him could forget that. Nor could he. "One day when Moses had grown up, he went out to his people and looked on their burdens, and he saw an Egyptian beating a Hebrew, one of his people. He looked this way and that, and seeing no one, he struck down the Egyptian and hid him in the sand" (Exodus 2:11–12).

Moses had been enculturated into the empire. Growing up in the palace, he absorbed the values and thought processes that belonged to imperial Egyptians. All that he had learned about solving problems he had learned from an empire that sought to solve the Hebrew problem by killing all the Hebrew boys, a fate Moses narrowly escaped. Empires solve their problems with coercion. One of the best forms of coercion available to the empire is violence. The empire considers the use of violence to protect its own people and place not only a right but even a responsibility.

So, Moses used his imperial problem-solving and killed the Egyptian. Problem solved. Temporarily.

> When he went out the next day, behold, two Hebrews were struggling together. And he said to the man in the wrong, "Why do you strike your companion?" He answered, "Who made you a prince and judge over us? Do you mean to kill me as you killed the Egyptian?" Then Moses was afraid, and thought, "Surely this thing is known." When Pharaoh heard of it, he sought to kill Moses. (Exodus 2:13–15)

Killing opponents, after all, is the empire's way.

But Moses was now confronted with a distressing reality about himself. He may have been a Hebrew, but he was not *habiru*. He was always a Hebrew! When he was in the palace, he was from the other side. When he was with Hebrews, he was still from the other side! He didn't belong with anyone.

Upon seeing his fellow Hebrew mistreated, Moses had made a conscious decision to reject the empire. But he found that rejecting the empire was a larger proposition than simply standing up for other Hebrews. As long as Moses used the tools and believed the philosophies of the empire, he would remain stuck in the empire.

Albert Einstein once observed, "No problem can be solved from the same level of consciousness that created it." If we use coercive violence to bring about the downfall of an oppressive empire, all we succeed in doing is creating a new oppressive empire. We may have good intentions of being benevolent this time, but history indicates it doesn't last. Of course, we will continue to think we are being benevolent, but the rest of the world knows otherwise. The problem is not solved.

Moses would need to find a new level of consciousness if he were going to actually help the *habiru* Hebrews and end their suffering under the empire. For the next forty years God would take Moses literally out into the middle of nowhere to have his imagination stretched into a new level of consciousness.

Anyone who lives meaningfully for the kingdom of God in this world of empires has, at some point, had to distance their thinking and imagination from the enculturation they have received within the empire. Both Egyptians and Hebrews had limited, imperial imaginations. When the Egyptians imagined what a better world would look like if everything were right, they imagined a bigger, more powerful, more prosperous Egyptian Empire. When the Hebrews imagined what a better world would look like, they imagined a strong, powerful Hebrew empire that would enslave the Egyptians and see how *they* felt about making bricks without being given any straw.

But what does God imagine when he imagines a better world?

Skipping over a number of fun stories including a walking stick that became a snake and parting the Red Sea, Moses went on to become leader of the nation God promised to Abraham. One of the first challenges to be faced was organizing a large community of slaves into people who could live together without foreign taskmasters telling them what to do.

God used Moses to give the children of Abraham a set of laws defining how this nation would live. Israel was designed to be unlike any other nation or empire on earth. It was to be an alternative to the self-protective, self-aggrandizing strategies of empires.

By this design, Israel would not have a king, a pharaoh, a caesar, or an emperor. The legal code would apply to everyone equally. The law made many provisions to ensure safety and equity for the stranger, the wanderer, and the sojourner. In the alternative way of living together God was building through Moses, the *habiru* would be treated with the exact standard of justice provided to a Jew of many generations.

There were also provisions in the law to protect people, especially the poor, from predatory economic practices. A wealthy person was to loan money out of compassion, not for profit. So, charging interest on a debt was forbidden. Within the law, the land itself would be treated with respect and not simply as a means to short-term economic growth. Every seven years the land was to be given a year of rest.

An even more significant law, especially for an agrarian society in which land provided security for future wealth, was that every fifty years land that had been sold was to be simply returned to its original owners. If one generation had to sell property to resolve a financial crisis, further generations would not be compromised by that loss. This would prevent the accumulation of huge wealth and property over many generations through inheritance.

If Israel would actually live by the provisions of the law of Moses, it would become an un-empire. It would provide all the nations of earth with a tangible, working example of how citizens can live together with equity for everyone, treating each person with equal justice and care.

These laws would be radical in the twenty-first century AD. Can you imagine the prospects of a political party that turned the law of Moses into an election platform? A vehement response, I fear, would come from the religious right. As radical as this is two millennia after Christ, imagine how radical it was two millennia before Christ!

The law of Moses is what it would have looked like to live under the kingdom of God in the world of ancient empires. And it hasn't changed much. But, as Jesus observed many years later, the children of Israel obeyed the law to the point of tithing their herb garden in the backyard "and have neglected the weightier matters of the law: justice and mercy and faithfulness" (Matthew 23:23). We have largely forgotten or discarded those issues in the law of Moses that would require us to live in community with complete equity. There are important theological reasons why a follower of Jesus is no longer bound to Jewish law. But Jesus compressed the principles underlying those laws into a single law for people wishing to live their lives under God's direction. We'll come to that!

In the meantime, North American Christians in today's global community are in exactly the same place Moses found himself having grown up in Pharaoh's palace. We don't belong to the empire. We belong to the kingdom of God. Or, as the apostle Paul put it, "We are fellow citizens with the saints and members of the household of God" (Ephesians 2:19). We are *Hebrew*, from the other side.

But, also like Moses, we are not *habiru*. We are not dusty and dirty. Despite the fact that we are from the other side, it is also true that growing up in Pharaoh's palace has left the values of the empire deeply embedded in our morals and philosophy. Part of us is always inclined to try to use the tools of the empire to impose the values of the kingdom on others.

Many centuries of Christendom have left the church in a position of power and wealth. It is a great temptation to use that power and wealth coercively. When we see an Egyptian taskmaster doing something we consider immoral, we strike him down. Moses used a sword, the tool of his empire. We use legislation, the tool of ours. But when we strike down the Egyptian oppressor, we are no further ahead. We are simply the Christian oppressor. An oxymoron, to be sure, but also a tragic historical reality.

God is capable of doing beyond what we could ask or imagine. But we are incapable of asking what we can't imagine, let alone committing ourselves to what we can't imagine. To carry his purposes forward through us, God is always looking for two qualities: great imagination and a corresponding desire to let God enliven our imaginations to his mission in the world.

Moses met these qualifications. His life had given him opportunity to view the world from multiple perspectives, a vital ingredient to social imagination. Of all the Hebrews in Egypt, Moses had the capacity to imagine the sort of society God wanted. Without this imagination Moses could not have welcomed God's law. For while God can act beyond our imagination, we cannot accept ideas beyond our imagination.

This is not to say that the community Moses envisioned was merely the product of his social/political imagination. Moses imagined in response to an encounter with God. The law is as much theological as it is social and political. Moses was able to imagine Abraham's children set free from slavery even when a realistic assessment would have concluded this was something Pharaoh never would allow.

The imagination of Moses left room for God to act in the world.

Christian imagination is informed by eschatology: a belief that God is not finished his creative activity in the world. We move toward an end in which Christ will return to earth and set things right. The nations will be healed! Every tribe and tongue will be brought together. Divisions will cease. This is the blessed hope.

As we wait in hope, imagining what our life together will be like in that great day, we are invited to begin living as if that day had already arrived. We know that the work of Christ is not yet fully realized in the world, but as his followers we can begin to live as an outpost of the world to come.

To live for the kingdom of God in the middle of any empire requires us to begin imagining a different way of living together: an alternative community. Within this imagined community—if our imagination is enlivened by God—there is welcome and safety for the *habiru* whose groaning God hears.

For the followers of Jesus, this alternative community has to begin in the church. To imagine such a church, we who are the church must face our complicity in the empire. We must stand above whatever Egyptian taskmaster we have slain and, realizing this is not God's way to solve the problem, repent of our use of the empire's tools and faithfulness to its ideals.

The empire we live in is as much economic as political and military. The nature of this empire leaves us vulnerable to the temptations of consumerism, triumphalism, and tribalism that are so often, and increasingly, seen in this empire. One of the most revealing questions we can ask ourselves is how we measure the church's success or effectiveness. The metric of the empire is wealth and expansion. What is God's metric for the church?

Could we imagine a church that measures its success by how kind it is to the dusty and dirty? Can we imagine a church that is moved by the same groans that move God? Can we imagine a church that lifts people up instead of striking them down?

Here is a hard truth. Much of the North American church is more attached to the empire than to God. We don't want to be. We just don't realize our situation. The king's palace feels like home.

This is why the church is such a brutal place for so many people. This explains why too often we experience church as a harsh and critical clique. It is time to reimagine our church life. What would it look like if the church were a place where people are welcomed into God's love rather than coerced into a prescribed pattern of morality? If the church really had an open door and a joyful welcome mat, who might actually come because they were finally unafraid of being rejected and condemned by the righteous?

One Sunday I was standing at the door after worship doing my pastoral duty, shaking hands with people as they left. A man who had been attending for some time greeted me with a smile and said, "I have finally decided."

"What have you decided?"

"I have decided to believe in Jesus."

Wow! I knew he had only been coming to church for his wife's sake. He was quite clear that he was not a believer. He was open to listen and discuss, and he had attended one of our Alpha courses to learn about faith, but nothing had moved him over that line of belief. I could hardly wait to see what point I had made in the sermon that finally convinced this intelligent and personable man to believe in Jesus! So, I asked him what had made the difference.

"I don't know if you noticed where we were sitting this morning. But right in front of us there was a guy. His arms are covered in tattoos. He smelled so strongly of alcohol that it almost made me dizzy. No one around seemed bothered by it. In fact, when we got up to shake hands and greet each other, a lot of people introduced themselves and told him they were happy to meet him and happy he had come. All the time you were speaking I was thinking of how sincere they seemed to be, and I decided the only explanation for this is that what this church believes is real."

Imagine that.

3

How Empires Get Into Us

My FATHER, WHO IS an avid sailor, has a simple principle for boating safety. "Keep the boat in the water, and keep the water out of the boat." Being a Jesus follower in the empire is much the same. It's not a bad thing to be in the empire. But it's a big problem if the empire begins to get into us.

It can be a good thing to be a Christian in the heart of the empire. Natives of the empire generally have resources and influence that are not shared by those colonized by the empire. When the empire is largely economic, this translates into financial resources that can be applied to the mission of the kingdom God is building.

Our challenge, however, is that, being reared in the empire, we are conditioned to accept the values and morality that created the empire in the first place. This blinds us to ways God would like to see our community transformed by alternative, and often opposing, values and morals.

Empires are careful to instill loyal and patriotic impulses in their citizens. Historically, empires have been very good at co-opting religious institutions and authorities into the cause of instilling such loyalty. Throughout Canada, for example, war memorials often contain the words "For God and King," as if one implies the other.

Religious commitment linked to an empire evokes loyalty that runs deeper than either emotion or intellect. Nations and empires consequently find religion a very helpful tool to keep people in line and civic morale high. When the empire is successful at co-opting religious institutions, religious people are not only in the empire, but the empire is in them. The empire becomes embedded in religious beliefs and ethics.

We skip quite a bit ahead in the biblical narrative to the Old Testament book of Daniel to see how this works and how we might respond to it. Daniel is set in a precarious time for the children of Abraham. The ten northern tribes, collectively known as Israel, had been captured and deported by the Assyrian Empire a little more than a century earlier. The southern tribes, collectively known as Judah, had aligned themselves with the Egyptian Empire. (Now there's a touch of irony!) King Jehoiakim of Judah governed as an Egyptian vassal.

In 605 BC Nebuchadnezzar, the king of Babylon, attacked Egyptian forces, defeating them at Carchemish. When he brought his forces into Judah, the king, Jehoiakim, abandoned his Egyptian masters and aligned himself with Nebuchadnezzar. He did, against the prophet Jeremiah's advice, reverse this decision three years later, with ultimately dire consequences. But in the meantime, Nebuchadnezzar had taken a number of Jewish nobles as hostages to the capital city of Babylon. As the book of Daniel begins, Daniel is serving Nebuchadnezzar's court in Babylon, another citizen of God's kingdom finding himself at the heart of an empire.

If you learned the story of Daniel in Sunday school or from *Veggie Tales*, you will recall Daniel had three friends who were thrown into a fiery furnace. As a brief Bible memory quiz, how many of Daniel's three friends can you name?

If you said Hananiah, Mishael, and Azariah, you're right! You're also pretty rare. Hardly anyone calls them by their real names. If, however, like most of us, you said Shadrach, Meshach, and Abednego, you're only partly right. The first chapter explains:

> The king commanded Ashpenaz, his chief eunuch, to bring some of the people of Israel, both of the royal

> family and of the nobility, youths without blemish and good appearance and skillful in all wisdom, endowed with knowledge, understanding, learning, and competent to stand in the king's palace, and to teach them the literature and language of the Chaldeans. The king assigned them a daily portion of the food that the king ate, and of the wine that he drank. They were to be educated for three years, and at the end of that time they were to stand before the king [as courtiers]. Among these were Daniel, Hananiah, Mishael, and Azariah of the tribe of Judah. And the chief of the eunuchs gave them names. Daniel he called Belteshazzar, Hananiah he called Shadrach, Mishael he called Meshach, and Azariah he called Abednego. (Daniel 1:3–7)

I don't know why we call Daniel by his Jewish name and the others by the names assigned by their Babylonian masters, but I'm pretty sure their mothers continued to call them Hananiah, Mishael, and Azariah.

Babylonian names were given to these young men as part of a larger program of enculturation into the Babylonian empire. Military power got these young men into the empire. It would take cultural conditioning to get the empire into Daniel, Hananiah, Mishael, and Azariah.

Canadians should be familiar with this strategy. Not very long ago we took children from indigenous parents and enrolled them in residential schools so we could teach them the literature and language of the British. We changed their beautiful names, such as Wâpanacâhkos (Cree for "Dawn Star"), into more Anglo names, such as Wilma or Wanda. And Wematin (Cree for "setting sun") we called William or Martin.

We did this because we were convinced, as are all empires, that the peoples we conquered would benefit by leaving behind their barbarian ways and finding their place in our clearly superior culture. The horrors of the residential school system in Canada simply reveal the hubris of empire and the danger that arrogance poses to the empire's vanquished subjects. To this day, Canada's first inhabitants remain second-class citizens.

But what can I do about it? I never sent anyone to a residential school! Yet, this is my history. I inherited it. What could Daniel's Babylonian neighbor have done other than respect and honor Daniel's true identity?

Notice that enculturation included learning new kinds of food. There would to be no more caribou and bannock for Daniel and his friends. From now on, it would be healthy food of the empire, such as roast beef and Yorkshire pudding. These young nobles had the honor of eating whatever was on the king's menu. The Babylonians were, quite literally, getting their empire into young people from conquered cultures.

Food is one of the main markers of culture. The best predictor of quality for any ethnic restaurant is to check the language spoken in the kitchen to see whether it matches the nationality advertised on the sign. It was the matter of food that led to Daniel's first firm resistance to enculturation. "Daniel resolved that he would not defile himself with the king's food, or with the wine that he drank" (Daniel 1:8).

There are a number of possible motives for Daniel's decision to decline the king's menu. Possibly he did not want to eat so richly when many of his people were living in poverty and deprivation. Perhaps Daniel and his friends felt it would defile them to benefit from the source of Jewish suffering.

Perhaps they objected because, as in many ancient cultures, the meat served at the table was first offered as a religious sacrifice. If this is the case, Daniel and his friends would not have wanted even passively to participate in a pagan religious practice. And certainly, if nothing else, the palace kitchen was not kosher.

Likely elements of all of these motives entered Daniel's mind. They add up to the same thing: Daniel did not want to eat what a Jew would not eat. He and his friends refused to have their identity stolen. It was bad enough that they had been taken from their homes. They were not going to let their homes be taken from their hearts.

Meanwhile, the Babylonians were equally keen to displace their Jewish identity. The stability and well-being of the empire required conquered foreigners to abandon their foreign ways and be absorbed into Babylonian life. Forcing people into a shared culture is not only a good way of nipping nationalistic or tribalistic uprisings in the bud, but it has the added benefit of enshrining in culture the knowledge that the empire's natives deserve to be in charge. They are exceptional. Their religion and values are clearly superior and more true than the misguided convictions of the conquered heathen.

A more severe test than the dinner menu was waiting for these young Jewish men. Nebuchadnezzar commissioned a ten-story golden sculpture, to which everyone was commanded to bow down and worship.

Empires love religion. One of the best ways to unite people is to give them a shared religion, while one of the best ways to control people is to give them a god who sees everything and punishes antisocial behavior. If the police don't catch you, God will! Even when an empire promotes atheism, it will promote that belief with great religious zeal—and it will attempt to restrain or retrain any religion that does not match the beliefs it wishes its subjects to share.

The sculpture commissioned by Nebuchadnezzar was unlikely to have been a statue celebrating the king's deity. That would have been more common in Egypt or Rome. It is more likely that this image was a pillar covered with inscriptions attributing god-like qualities to Nebuchadnezzar. Instead of proclaiming the king divine, it more likely merely identified Nebuchadnezzar as the best and most direct connection the empire had to God. Honor to the king was not only a civic duty but a spiritual responsibility as well.

If the king exhibits divine qualities, we might not understand his edicts, but we can be assured they are the gods' will. The gods do many things we don't understand, but we don't rebel against them because of it. If the empire does something truly awful, violent, and brutal, well, sometimes a god is harsh and demanding. Those who stand in a god's way or seek to thwart his will should not be surprised if the response is viciously punitive.

Being one so close to his god, or perhaps being a god himself, a king has a divine right to do and decide as he pleases. He cannot be held to same standard as everyone else. He is on a different level. The king's actions cannot be judged by mere mortals.

Nebuchadnezzar did not succeed in transplanting this spirituality into Hananiah, Mishael, and Azariah. Because these Jewish students would not worship the image, they were thrown into a fiery furnace as a cautionary tale for others. But the fire did not consume them. In fact, the king thought he could see someone who truly was like a god in the furnace with them.

> Nebuchadnezzar came near to the door of the burning fiery furnace . . . and said, "Blessed be the God of Shadrach, Meshach, and Abednego, who has sent his angel and delivered his servants who trusted in him, and set aside the king's command, and yielded up their bodies rather than serve and worship any god other than their own God. Therefore I make a decree. Any people, nation, or language that speaks anything against the God of Shadrach, Meshach, and Abednego shall be torn limb from limb, and their houses laid in ruins, for there is no other god who is able to rescue in this way." (Daniel 3:26, 28–29)

Isn't this wonderful! The emperor of Babylon was converted to the God of the Bible! In fact, he even became an evangelist for the Jewish God, lifting God's reputation among all tribes and nations. It may be that his methods of persuasion still needed conversion, but how else would a person in his position make his case for God?

Unless this wasn't so much of a spiritual conversion as a political flip-flop. By the next chapter of Daniel, Nebuchadnezzar will be claiming divine glory again. The whole fiery-furnace thing had been just a setback in his self-deification.

It is the first choice of an empire to enculturate captured people out of their own religion and into the empire's religion. But if that doesn't work, the second-best strategy is to coopt the religion of resistant populations as an ally favored by the empire. This is achieved by using the language and rituals of the co-opted religion to sanctify the power of the empire. This does not, however, extend to the empire being guided by the actual values of that religion. If the empire can't get religion out of its conquered subjects, it can always get the empire into the religion of those subjects.

The empire claims God without following God. In fact, the empire manages this dissonance by changing God into something more malleable to the empire's needs.

The Roman Empire did this very successfully seventeen hundred years ago. Unable to eradicate Christians who refused to be enculturated into the religion of ancient Rome, Rome coopted the church, giving it great wealth and political power, but thus robbing it of spiritual power for nearly two millennia. There is an apocryphal story about a saint visiting medieval Rome. Having shown all the beautiful art and wealth of the church to the saint, the pope concluded, "No longer can we say with the apostles, 'Silver and gold have we none.'"

"No," said the saint, "But nor can we say to the lame, 'In the name of Jesus of Nazareth, get up and walk!'"

The church had moved from healing the lives of ordinary people to undergirding the wealth and power of an elite. It was no longer the church of Jesus. This should not be understood as a problem exclusive to Roman Catholics. Protestant megachurches dotting the North American landscape quite often make a show of their gold and silver. Indeed, the more gold and silver we have collected, the more we assume God is blessing our ministry. See what wonderful towers we have built for him!

We have built steeples to rival the Tower of Babel. And what a name we have made for ourselves!

When we design an image of God to meet our needs, this is called idolatry. We are replacing the God Who Is with a more comfortable image of him. There are three theological themes that will almost always emerge in the formal, accepted religion of the empire as the empire describes God in ways that promote socialization into the empire's culture.

First, the empire needs a God who is punitive. The threat of divine punishment can be an even better deterrent to crime and rebellion than the threat of civil punishment. The empire can lock us away or even execute us. But God can condemn us for eternity, whether or not the authorities ever catch up with us.

A second theological theme in imperial religion is an individualized, personal focus on morality rather than on mysticism. The God of the empire is concerned about concrete conformity to expected behaviors. Morality is personal, not collective. The government will look after economic systems, while religion will regulate people's sex lives. God is concerned about whether we cheat or steal, not whether our society is racist or unjust. God, and therefore God's servants, are never critical of the empire.

Third, the empire's god is very critical of other empires and worldviews. God is a tribal mascot for one group of people among all the various nations, tribes, and empires competing for wealth and power. God is for "us and our ways" and is against "them and their ways." As an ultimate sign of displeasure with those who do not worship the god of the empire, the empire may well go to war in god's name and for god's glory to defeat and displace "their" unbelief and disobedience.

If this seems to describe a lot of classical Christianity, it should be remembered that most of Christian history occurred in the age of Christendom, in which the church walked hand in hand with one empire or another. The doctrine of the divine right of kings is a theological indication of how closely the church walked with the king.

The first written expression of this doctrine was penned (and there is no surprise here) by a king: James VI of Scotland. His *Basilikon Doron* was written as an instruction manual for his young son to absorb while growing into his eventual reign. The notion is simple: the king is king because God ordained it to be so. The king therefore speaks for God on earth. To obey the king is to obey God. To disobey the king is to disobey God. To die for the king is to die for God. Hence, we mark the graves of fallen soldiers with the words "For God and King." The two are indissoluble.

Strangely enough, when James VI wrote his advice to his son, Scotland considered its king to be only "the first among equals" with his fellow nobles. The divine right of kings reshaped that political landscape.

Stranger yet, the doctrine continues to persist even in democratic contexts where the monarch is only figurative, or where there is no monarch at all. One of many examples of contemporary takes on the divine right of kings came shortly after the 2016 presidential election in the United States, when a number of prominent evangelical leaders declared that Donald Trump was chosen by God to be president. We can't help but notice how quickly this doctrine is forgotten when another party or ideology comes into power.

Biblical faith does not sanction the empire. Any empire.

The empire is most powerful when it gets into us: when it moves beyond military or economic conquest and becomes a set of beliefs and values. Framed in any religion, these are the underlying values of the empire that are embedded in the culture of the empire:

- The world is divided between "us" and "them."

- The only way we can be safe from "them" is to dominate them. If we do not achieve dominance, we will be dominated.

- Our peace and security rely on military, economic, educational, and religious institutions to support one another.

- Our society is clearly superior to other societies. When we force other societies to follow our rules and beliefs, we are doing them a favor for which we may be proud and they should be grateful.

These values are supported by a theology that may be built around the rituals and beliefs of any particular religion:

- God is on our side. To oppose us is evil. To support us is wise and good.

- God punishes the wicked. To oppose us elicits God's condemnation. To join us is to join the true God.

- The government, its laws, and its agents are ordained by God. Other societies might have evil laws, but it displeases God when people break our laws.

- The world would be a better and safer place if everyone believed exactly what we believe in the way we believe it.

- It is not only our right to tell other people how they should live. It is our responsibility.

Daniel and his friends could not help being taken into the heart of the empire. But they firmly resisted allowing the empire into their hearts. They refused to be co-opted and absorbed into the empire's culture. They rejected the attempt to foist empire theology upon them.

They had one advantage I don't have. They didn't grow up in the empire. They had already experienced an alternative. They had read the words of prophets who warned about the dangers of empire, and even how their own Jewish nation often committed idolatry and welcomed the pagan beliefs of empire into Judaism. They began life standing outside the empire.

I began standing inside the empire. Each of the beliefs I listed above is something I at one time believed. I believed it because the version of Christianity I first experienced had been redacted by nearly two thousand years of Christian empires. It was only Jesus as he speaks and acts in the Gospels who began to offer an alternative theology and morality to me.

We will not advance with the kingdom of God unless we critically assess the beliefs we inherited from Christendom.

4

Empire in God's Name

MY SON'S CLOSEST FRIEND in high school, Dave, was enamored with a television cartoon called *Pinky and the Brain*. For the uninitiated, Pinky and the Brain were lab rats with projects of their own that began every night after the scientists hung their lab coats on the wall and went home. Each episode began with this exchange:

Pinky: "Gee, Brain, what do you want to do tonight."

Brain: "The same thing we do every night, Pinky—try to take over the world!"

Having never seen the cartoon, but hearing the boys mimic this conversation on a regular basis, one evening I asked, "Why do the Brain and Pinky want to take over the world?"

Dave looked at me in amazement. "Mr. Tempelmeyer! Why *wouldn't* you want to take over the world!?"

Why not, indeed?

I have to admit that I have quite often said the world would be a much happier place if everyone just did what I said they should do. I was joking, but the truth is: on a case-by-case basis, I kind of believe this to be true. A more rational part of me knows that it is not, but that's what I feel.

"Go therefore and make disciples of all nations, baptizing them in the name of the Father, the Son, and the Holy Spirit, teaching them to observe all I have commanded you" (Matthew 28:27–28). Isn't this command we like to call the Great Commission a form of world conquest?

I've written about Nimrod in Shinar, Pharaoh in Egypt, and Nebuchadnezzar in Babylon. Empire builders, yes. But these were bad empires. Pharaoh, Nebuchadnezzar, Caesar Augustus: these were bad emperors. They worked against God. They oppressed God's people. They were idolaters.

But couldn't we build an empire *for* the true God? If we could take over the world and create an empire dedicated to doing God's work and will, wouldn't that be a good thing? A good thing for God, a good thing for the world, and if it happened to be a good thing for us, well, that would just be a happy coincidence.

A key to interpreting the Bible is understanding that the Bible gives us a history of a community of people who believed in God. The Bible provides a record of how these people worked out their faith in the world and how that worked for the world and for them. The narrative is unflinching in recording the mistakes these people sometimes made. We would know the Bible better if we were as unflinching in acknowledging these mistakes as mistakes. Within this history of people working out their faith together, there is an example of an empire built with the intention of serving God and promoting his work in the world.

Both Jewish and Christian thinkers tend to view this time as a highlight of the Old Testament period. We consider the people who made this effort heroic and wise. It is therefore counterintuitive to take an honest and critical look at their empire. But if we are to be faithful to God we need to study the Scriptures openly, willing to discern and learn from the good, the bad, and the ugly.

Here's how the holy Jewish empire began.

> When Samuel became old, he made his sons judges over Israel . . . Yet his sons did not walk in his ways but turned aside after gain. They took bribes and perverted justice.
> Then all of the elders of Israel gathered together and came to Samuel at Ramah and said to him, "Behold, you are old and your sons do not walk in your ways. Now

appoint for us a king to judge us like the other nations."
(1 Samuel 8:1–5)

What could be gained from having the kind of king and governance found in the nations around Israel? From their inception in Shinar, empires have sought to constantly expand their military and economic supremacy as a strategy for protecting their own people and what they already have. At least as they climb toward the peak of their power, one positive observation can be made about empires: they *do* protect their own people and what they own, at least for a limited period of time.

There are efficiencies in an empire. We can travel throughout the Mediterranean world today and still see remains of viaducts and bridges that were built by the Romans. One factor contributing to the rapid spread of the gospel of Jesus was Pax Romana: the safety that military occupation provided to people traveling around the Roman Empire. It is commonly said of Mussolini, the World War II dictator of Italy, that, if nothing else, under his rule at least the trains ran on time.

Military and economic supremacy not only offer benefits to the empire's citizens, but could be used to promote the kingdom of God. Why wouldn't you want to take over the world!?

Despite the potential benefits, God suggested through Samuel that the people of Israel might want to think twice about coronating a king. The rule of unintended consequences was bound to play havoc with the ultimate outcome.

> The Lord said to Samuel, "Obey the voice of the people in all that they say to you, for they have not rejected you, but they have rejected me from being king over them . . . Obey their voice; only you shall solemnly warn them and show them the ways of the king who shall reign over them."
>
> So Samuel told all the words of the Lord to the people who were asking for a king from him. He said, "These will be the ways of the king who will reign over you: he will take your sons and appoint them to his chariots and to be his horsemen and to run before his chariots. And he will appoint for himself commanders of thousands

and commanders of fifties, and some to plow his ground and to reap his harvest, and to make his implements of war and the equipment of his chariots. He will take your daughters to be perfumers and cooks and bakers. He will take the best of your fields and vineyards and olive orchards and give them to his servants. He will take the tenth of your grain and of your vineyards and give it to his officers and to his servants. He will take your male servants and female servants and the best of your young men and your donkeys, and put them to his work. He will take the tenth of your flocks, and you shall be his slaves. And in that day you will cry out because of your king, whom you have chosen for yourselves, but the Lord will not answer you in that day." (1 Samuel 8:7, 9–18)

The people had considered some of the benefits enjoyed by nations under a monarchy, but they had not anticipated some of the costs. The most severe cost comes with the assumption that they had merely rejected a system of government. In fact, they had rejected a unique relationship with God, who had rescued them from slavery and created from them an alternative to the world's empires. They thought a human king would do a better job of taking care of them than the God who led them out of Egypt into a land of plenty.

But this is only one of the costs. Their sons would be drafted into the military. Weren't they already being drafted into the military? No, that is not how the children of Israel's society had been structured by the law of Moses.

Empires require a standing military. But the tribes of Israel were farmers. If an enemy attacked one part of the family, some or all of the other tribes would temporarily leave the farm, go to the defense of those under attack, and when the threat was over, go back to the farm.

These temporary military engagements were not led by a cadre of trained military officers. When such leadership was needed, the Spirit of God thrust forward a charismatic leader or judge to organize resistance to the threat. If this seems like a path to certain defeat, the lack of military culture was offset by the knowledge that Israel did not fight alone. God was an ally in battle and would bring victory in surprising and unconventional ways. Israel's survival had always been due to the acts of God rather than the strength of an army.

Beyond a standing military, a monarchy would imply a more significant change: an inevitable stratification of social class. Some people would live in palaces. Other people would be required to serve the needs of the fortunate ones inhabiting these palaces. Land ownership would be accessible only at the pleasure of the king. The king could take from those who displeased him and give it as a reward to those who did please him. This despite the law of Moses, which provided that land would be returned to its original owners every fifty years.

The implementation of a Jewish monarchy in Israel would entail a complete rejection of the social equity imagined and provided by the law of Moses. Even if a Jewish pharaoh is Jewish, he is still, after all, a pharaoh.

The first king of the tribes of Israel was named Saul. He was what is expected of a king, at least on the surface. Tall and handsome, he looked like a man born for leadership. This is not to say he was without flaw. He was a little bit insane, somewhat sociopathic. But truthfully, this is not always a disadvantage for kings or emperors. In fact, a number of people who have run empires have been good at it precisely because they were a little bit sociopathic. This characteristic helped them remain focused on the advancement of the empire rather than becoming distracted by the way a few people were getting run over by it.

The next king was David. It was under David that the kingdom really began to get some traction as a minor empire. David expanded the territory of the twelve tribes. He conquered a number of enemies that had plagued the tribes prior to his leadership. David was a military man, and very good at it.

He was also good at accumulating wealth in the process of accumulating territory. Not only did the nation gain prosperity through his rule, but his own tribe of Judah and his own family did very well while he was on the throne. Such great wealth flowed into the tribe of Judah that it became the dominant tribe of Israel. (To this day, all Jews are named for Judah.)

It should be acknowledged that King David committed some sexual improprieties and used his office to end the life of a lover's husband. But a touch of scandal and what intelligence services like to call "dark ops" are almost always overlooked as long as a leader is able to keep the trains running on time and the economy ticking along.

David was followed by his son Solomon. The Jewish empire reached the apex of its power, territorial control, and wealth during the reign of Solomon. Military and economic success marked his era.

Given his success as king, it is surprising that this is not what is best known about Solomon. If we were to randomly ask people in church what they know about Solomon, they would probably give two answers. He had the reputation for being the wisest man on earth. And he had a harem of approximately one thousand wives and concubines.

The reason for such a large harem was political. Solomon used marriage as a way of sealing alliances that would protect his power and stretch his empire. As his reach grew broader, the foreign convictions of his many wives and concubines eventually carried Solomon away from his faithfulness to God. Perhaps I'm missing something, but this does not seem wise to me!

When Solomon died and his son Rehoboam came to the throne, it was time to pay the piper. Solomon had built magnificent imperial infrastructure in Jerusalem: palaces, stables, an expanded wall, and so on. All of these structures needed staff to fulfill their usefulness to the empire. Solomon was able to stay ahead of it by enlarging territory and wealth. But the kingdom of Judah was beginning to push at the borders of Egypt to the southwest and Babylon to the northeast. There wasn't much more room for wealth through conquest and expansion.

The only way Rehoboam could pay the bills was through heavily taxing the people. This was difficult enough for the two tribes of Israel (Judah and Benjamin) at the southern end of the kingdom. But for the ten northern tribes it felt intolerable. At least the southerners could enjoy some of the benefits by being near Jerusalem, but all the northerners could see was their money headed south to keep Judah magnificent.

The hardship and bitterness of this taxation provoked a movement toward northern independence that culminated in the northern tribes selecting their own king. In only four generations the people had become exhausted by all the specific things Samuel had warned them about. From this time on the twelve tribes of Israel were divided, the ten northern tribes being known as Israel while the southern tribes retained the name Judah.

A number of kings followed on both sides of the border. Some were good and influenced the people to move toward God and the kind of life that had been envisioned under the law of Moses. Others were bad and influenced both nations to turn away from the God of Abraham and Moses and follow other ancient Near Eastern deities.

Weakened by division into two nations and with the erosion of its identity as an alternative community of God, the Jewish empire imploded. Both nations became increasingly vulnerable to neighboring empires. The long-term impact of Rehoboam's taxation to pay for his father's projects was the defeat of both nations: the disappearance of the northern tribes through absorption into the Assyrian Empire, and the Jewish people remaining under foreign rule for many centuries to come.

We see the law of unintended consequences continue to work through David and Solomon in the construction of the temple in Jerusalem. This was initially David's idea. But when David discussed this with Nathan, a prophet, after Nathan had prayed he brought a clear message from God to the King.

> Go and tell my servant David, "Thus says the Lord: Would you build me a house to dwell in? I have not lived in a house since the day I brought up the people of Israel from Egypt to this day, but I have been moving about in a tent for my dwelling. In all places where I have moved with all the people of Israel, did I speak a word with any

of the judges of Israel, whom I commanded to shepherd
my people Israel, saying, "Why have you not built me a
house of cedar?"' (2 Samuel 7:4–7)

God was no more keen for Israel to have a temple than he was
for them to have a king. He made it clear that he did not need a
temple. He is God; his glory is not reliant on what humans build
for him. He said he had never asked anyone to build a temple for
him because he did not want a permanent dwelling.

When David became king, the religion of Israel belonged to
the people. The priestly tribe of Levi had been given no land in the
settlement of Israel because they were to be scattered all across the
nation to serve God and people in whatever towns and villages
they happened to live. God was happy to be where people were.
He was happy to move in the rhythms of ordinary daily lives in
ordinary communities wherever his people happened to be.

The tabernacle described in the law of Moses was a tent. The
wonderful thing about a tent is that it does not confine the presence of God to one fixed place. It is portable. The tabernacle was a
metaphor that God can go anywhere he pleases. He is expected to
be on the move. He is free.

Empires do not like a free God. A free God might criticize the
empire. A free God might declare prophecies through male and female servants rather than through the proper channels of authority and responsibility. Even though David and Solomon wanted
to honor God in building a temple, they were thinking like other
nations who served other gods. Just as when the people asked for
a king in the first place.

In God's rejection of David's plan for a temple, the news was
not all bad. Nathan continued,

Moreover, the Lord declares to you that the Lord will
make you a house. When your days are fulfilled and you
lie down with your fathers, I will raise up your offspring
after you, who shall come from your body, and I will
establish his kingdom. He shall build a house for my
name, and I will establish the throne of his kingdom

forever. I will be to him a father, and he shall be to me a
son. (2 Samuel 7:10–14)

This promise is theologically profound. There is so much in these
few verses to contemplate. While God had no need for David to
build a house of God, God wanted to build a house for David.
God, as he is found in the Bible, loves to give. But the "house"
God would give to David was not to be a structure made of wood
or stone. It would be a person. This person would have a kingdom that was not an empire. And this person would be a temple: a
dwelling place for God, a holy of holies where God could be found
in all his fullness.

Many years later Jesus and his disciples were walking past
the magnificent temple being constructed by Herod. The disciples
were enthralled with its beauty, majesty, and glory. Jesus responded
to their admiration of the temple by announcing that he would destroy the temple and raise it back up in three days. This was clearly
absurd. Herod's temple had already been decades under construction and still wasn't finished.

It was only later the disciples recognized Jesus was talking
about his body. His body was the temple. His body was the house
promised to David. And through the death and resurrection of
that body, God was going to be set free again.

On the day Jesus died, the Gospel reports there was an earth-
quake that caused the heavy fabric curtain separating the holy of
holies from the rest of the temple to be ripped in two. The only
place on earth ancient Jews believed the full presence of God could
be found was in the room behind this curtain. It was an intersec-
tion between heaven and earth. Only the most spiritually elite ever
entered, and then only once a year. God was being kept in solitary
confinement.

The tearing of the curtain was perhaps not so much about
letting people in as letting God back out! God would no longer be
confined to one room in one building. He would go wherever he
wished, just as the wind blows where it wills. He would fill people
with his Holy Spirit, and his temple would be multiplied all over

the earth in every tribe and nation. His temple would stand as an alternative to empires of the world and their idolatries.

It should be noted that empires can make lovely religion. When David centralized the religious life of Israel into Jerusalem, the music and liturgy were incredibly beautiful, so beautiful that we still use its songbook today. The celebrations were so attractive and compelling that people came from literally miles around to be part of the festivities. Then they went back to their ordinary lives, leaving God confined to his quarters.

At least God had the prophets through whom he spoke his critique of life in the empire. He critiqued the social inequities. He critiqued the lovely, beautiful worship that came from people's lips but did not touch them in a way they would begin to feed the poor and needy and to love the nations God longed to draw to himself. The kings heard the words of the prophets. And more often than not their response was to silence God's voice through imprisoning and killing God's prophets. Empires like religion, but only when it is under imperial control.

It is possible, nevertheless, for religious leaders to thrive in the empire. Religion near the heart of the empire has resources, unlike religion in other places. Religious leaders acting on the values and strategies of empire have plenty of money to build great churches: beautiful cathedrals with excellent music and art. People will come for miles around. But because the empire has found its way into religion, it is the empire that finds its way into people's hearts. Not God.

There is an ugly side even to the temple of Jerusalem. This is how building such a magnificent edifice was accomplished:

> King Solomon drafted forced labor out of all Israel, and the draft numbered 30,000 men. And he sent them to Lebanon, 10,000 a month in shifts. They would be a month in Lebanon and two months at home. Adoniram was in charge of the draft. Solomon also had 70,000 burden-bearers and 80,000 stonecutters in the hill country, besides Solomon's 3,300 chief officers who were over the work, who had charge of the people who carried on the work. (1 Samuel 5:13–16)

Why do we overlook Solomon's use of forced labor when we talk about the temple? Could it be that to acknowledge this detail would bring into question God's place in the building?

This detail deserves some reflection. God had heard the groaning of the children of Israel when they were forced into labor to build monuments for Pharaoh. And now the children of Israel were forced into labor again to build a temple for Solomon. Was God deaf to their groans? Was this acceptable because the people were being coerced by a Jewish king into building something for God? Even if the pharaoh is Jewish, he is still a pharaoh.

But as Samuel warned, when the empire gets into the people of God, "The Lord will not hear you on that day." God can't save us when we are busy trying to save ourselves. God can't save us when we have rejected the assumption that our salvation is found in becoming faithful to his ways.

The kingdom of God cannot be built with the tools and strategies of empire building. When out of good intentions Christians try to use imperial means to build God's kingdom, we merely become Christian pharaohs.

This happened in Puritan Massachusetts. It happened when John Calvin tried to coerce Geneva to fulfill his vision of a godly community and was driven out of the city. It continues to happen as the religious right in North America lends support to immoral leadership because that leadership promises power to the evangelical community.

There are many good and deeply committed Christians who serve in political office because they care about their community. This does not mean that the mere fact someone is a Christian makes them worthy of our vote. There is no indication that a nation led by Christians is, at the end of the day, any holier than a nation led by Buddhists, Muslims, or atheists.

What makes a politician worthy of our vote is the policy they intend to implement and their willingness to be a public servant for the common good—not just for our good. The nature of the political enterprise in democratic societies requires a certain amount of expedient compromise. A politician worthy of our vote will engage in this process with integrity and great willingness to listen to all the voices discussing what the common good requires. That means they will listen to and seek the good of people who are Christians and those who are not: people who do not share Christian faith and values alongside people who do.

The mindset of empire has so entered the North American Christian mind that we actively seek civic leaders willing to impose our values on people who do not share these values. I suspect this is largely because we have not been able to persuade our culture to embrace our values. Having enjoyed the era of Christendom, when we could assume everyone was bound together by Judeo-Christian values, it is easier to enforce those values than to articulate what lies behind them in a persuasive way.

If we want to live for the kingdom from the middle of an empire, we must renounce the tools and strategies the empire has developed to get its way.

Many Protestants quickly see how the papacy arose as an attempt to build an empire for God. We are much slower to see how church life in North America is governed by the same impulse to build ecclesiastical empires.

A church, pastor, or ministry can never be evaluated by how big it is or how much money it generates. Our religious life has become divided by walls, preoccupied with expansion, and impressed with wealth. Entrepreneurial pastors have built empires the same way multinational corporations have built empires. Everyone knows Pharaoh's name.

I decided some years ago that I will never again buy or read a book that advertises the size of the author's congregation on the back cover. This is not because I believe such an author is incapable of writing a good book. It is because it is a sign of ill health bordering on idolatry to use such a metric to validate a writer's work. If enough of us stop playing the game, perhaps the church as a whole will find a more reasonable metric to evaluate worth.

Ministries often follow a predictable trajectory. A person, moved by the Holy Spirit, engages in ministry in a fresh way. The empowering of the Spirit causes this movement to grow, and others to begin to implement similar ministry in their own place. And the Spirit moves through the movement.

But at some point, the originating ministry begins to adapt the tools of today's business empires to promote the work. The originating ministry shifts from a movement to a machine designed to expand the empire. Nothing drives the Holy Spirit from a ministry faster than trying to become a religious empire. Unfortunately, the efficiencies found in the empire mindset continue to provide attention, money, and attraction. It may be that no one even notices the Holy Spirit has left, because the machine is still drawing crowds and enthusiasm.

If you really want to know how much a church or ministry is moving in God, don't look at the size or beauty of its building. Don't consider the attractiveness and popularity of its leader.

Look at how that church or ministry welcomes the *habiru*, the "dusty and dirty." Do rich and poor meet together as equal brothers and sisters in the family of God? Are people invited to participate because they vibrate with the love of God rather than because of how they contribute to the production value of an event? Are diverse races and cultures coming together as one in Christ? Not just in the pews, but also in the boardroom and the staff meeting?

David wanted to build a house for God. God wanted to build a house for David. Why wouldn't we want to take over the world? Why wouldn't we want to build an empire for God? Because God is already building a kingdom for us.

5

Empire and the Cross

IN MY SUNDAY SERMON the week after Nelson Mandela died, I offered him as an example of the kingdom of God working in our world. Like many churches, our church served coffee and snacks after worship. This time provides people an opportunity for fellowship alongside an opportunity to correct the morning sermon. A friend from South Africa made use of this opportunity to inquire whether I really thought kingdom work could be accomplished by a terrorist.

From my standpoint, Nelson Mandela was a courageous hero. But from the standpoint of my friend, whose family left South Africa during the unsettled final years of apartheid, Nelson Mandela was a violent terrorist. When I took a deeper look at the actual history, I had to acknowledge that both points of view contain some validity.

If you happened to be a Roman in AD 35, how do you think you would have viewed Jesus, the carpenter-preacher from a small Jewish town?

During the early years of the church, why was the Roman Empire so concerned about the spread of Christianity? Many other religions and philosophies were spreading across the Roman Empire at the time as Pax Romana provided a relative degree of safety for travelers, which in turn permitted a wide exchange of beliefs and ideas. Most of these beliefs and ideas were not troubling to the authorities. So why did the Roman authorities try to suppress Christianity?

Were they concerned about questions of religious truth? Were they offended that so many were disregarding traditional homage to Roman gods and goddesses?

Or were they worried that a large majority of the people turning to Christianity were slaves and others at the bottom rungs of the social order? Were they concerned that the very people whose backs carried the weight of Roman society were denying Caesar's claims to deity and preaching about a king more powerful even than death? Did Roman authorities view Christianity as a religious threat or a political threat?

A congregant recently asked: "I understand why it was necessary for Jesus to die, but why did God need him to die in such a brutal way? Why did God need something like the cross?" That's a very good question! We should recall on what charge Jesus of Nazareth was arrested and executed.

The nature of Jesus' execution reveals a great deal about the underlying meaning of his death. The Romans executed many people and were quite creative in inventing ways to turn public executions into compelling social theater. Execution by crucifixion was exclusively reserved for only two classes of people: slaves and political insurgents. The violence and humiliation of the cross was a way of demonstrating the absolute contempt with which the Roman rulers held these particular people.

When the Jewish leaders brought Jesus before the Roman governor, Pontius Pilate, this is the charge they brought against him: "We found this man subverting our nation, opposing payment of taxes to Caesar, and saying that he, himself, is the Messiah, a king" (Luke 23:2 CSB).

After examining Jesus regarding this charge, Pilate told the Jewish leaders that, though they had brought Jesus to him as one who "subverts the people," he could find no evidence to support this charge. They insisted Jesus was guilty of the capital offense of rejecting Roman authority and stirring up the people to do the same.

I don't mean to dismiss or diminish the spiritual significance of the cross. However, that spiritual meaning cannot be fully appreciated without also understanding that, to the people of Jerusalem on the day of his execution, the death of Jesus was a political event. Jesus was a political prisoner executed by the state on the charge of sedition. That is why he was executed on a cross, and that is why God needed him to die such a death. In the years following his death, many of his followers also died as political prisoners executed on the basis of the same charge.

At the cross of Jesus we see most starkly the contrast between the kingdom of God and the empires of the world. On the cross the Son of God was put to death in the name of law and order.

In the months leading up to his arrest and death, Jewish leaders argued about how they should respond to the threat Jesus posed to the existing order. Some were concerned about ways the Jesus movement could place the whole nation in danger. "If we let him go on like this," they said, "the Romans will come and take away our place and nation." The chief priest offered a solution along with a justification for that solution: "It is better for you that one man should die for the people, not that the whole nation should perish" (John 11:50).

To frame these words within the concept of civil rights would be to ignore the different historical context in which this debate took place. But if this discussion had occurred in our present context, the argument of the chief priest would have been, "If we have to ignore the civil rights of one person to protect the peace, stability, and security of the whole nation, then that is what we need to do." Jesus had become a political problem not only for the Romans, but also for his own Jewish people.

The conflict between kingdom and empire came to a head when Jesus faced Pilate, whose approval was required before an execution could take place. Pilate was trying to understand the obviously absurd claim that this Jewish peasant was threatening to overpower the empire.

> So Pilate entered his headquarters again and called Jesus and said to him, "Are you the King of the Jews?"
>
> Jesus answered, "Do you say this of your own accord, or did others say it to you about me?"
>
> Pilate answered, "Am I a Jew? Your own nation and the chief priests have delivered you over to me. What have you done?"
>
> Jesus answered, "My kingdom is not of this world. If my kingdom were of this world, my servants would have been fighting, that I might not be delivered over to the Jews. But my kingdom is not from the world."
>
> Then Pilate said to him, "So you are a king?"
>
> Jesus answered, "You say that I am a king. For this purpose I was born and for this purpose I have come into the world—to bear witness to the truth." (John 18:33–37)

"If my kingdom were of this world, my servants would have been fighting . . . But my kingdom is not from the world." Was Jesus identifying a geographical problem faced by his servants? Was he implying they were simply too far away to fight in his defense, but if they could have arrived in time they certainly would have kept his arrest and execution from happening?

Or was Jesus suggesting a more fundamental distance than geography? Was he saying, "If my kingdom operated by the same principles, policies, and strategies as those that have arisen in the empires of the world, then my servants would have used their supernatural powers to fight for and secure my release. But my kingdom operates on a whole different set of principles, policies, and strategies. My kingdom is never the product of violence, nor is violence ever the means by which my kingdom is victorious."

During my student days I lived in the neighborhood of Toronto known as Greektown. My daily commute took me past several butcher shops displaying meat hanging in the front window. As Easter neared, these Greek butchers featured whole lambs hanging in the window, still wearing a wool coat with a reddish-brown stain at the neck where the slaughtered lambs had been bled.

Where I grew up meat came from foam trays wrapped in cellophane. I have to confess these bloody lambs hanging in the window were quite unsettling for me.

At the time, my favorite metaphor for Christ was the Lion of Judah. I am a big fan of C. S. Lewis's Chronicles of Narnia. The dignity and power of Aslan combined with the notion of the regal lion as animal king seemed to speak perfectly of the power and majesty of King Jesus.

It came as something of a surprise to learn that the image of the Lion of Judah only appears one time in the Bible. A closer look at the text was even more surprising. It is found in the highly pictorial, symbolic book, Revelation. John, the Revelator, was found weeping because no one was able to open an important scroll. "And one of the elders said to me, 'Weep no more; behold, the Lion of the tribe of Judah, the Root of David, has conquered, so that he can open the scroll'" (Revelation 5:5).

Revelation speaks in pictures, so when John is told to behold—to look—we are about to see a word picture describing this Lion of the tribe of Judah. John tells us what he saw: "I saw a Lamb standing, as though it had been slain . . . And he went and took the scroll" (Revelation 5:6–7).

Apparently, the Lion of Judah does not look at all like the drawing of Aslan on the front cover of *The Lion, the Witch, and the Wardrobe*. In fact, the Lion of Judah actually looks much more like one of the dead lambs hanging by its hindquarters in Greektown. With its coat of wool stained reddish-brown by its many wounds, the Lamb that was slain has returned to life, his death wounds still obvious.

The victorious Lion of Judah who has conquered is still clearly weak, vulnerable, and wounded. This is because the Lion of Judah does not obtain victory by inflicting wounds and death but by absorbing wounds and death. The greatest glory of Christ is his willingness to be obedient and vulnerable to death, even to death on a cross: the chosen form of Roman execution for political insurgents.

What if an angelic army had come to rescue Jesus from Pilate and the Jewish court? Not stopping there, what if this angelic army had proceeded to demolish the Roman forces, finally enthroning Jesus in the heart of Rome, surrounded by his servants, willing to fight?

We would still be lost in a world of violence and coercion. This is simply another way of saying we would still be lost in our sin. What God accomplished through Jesus could only be accomplished by willingness to suffer and die in the face of violence, brutality, and the expedience of the empire.

On the cross Jesus not only offered a perfectly obedient humanity to God; he also offered a perfect divine protest against the violence and division created by empire. The cross is, at one time, a sacrifice in heaven and a political upheaval on earth. The cross is not an appeal to an angry God. The cross is God's appeal to an angry world.

While still alive, Jesus said many things about the kingdom of God. He said it is here, it is among us, it is not only near us, but even within us if we can only grasp it. We will know it is working when sick people are healed and when people captive to evil are freed to live ordinary and constructive lives. We see this kingdom when the poor, who so often hear only bad news about how human powers and authorities are working, will finally receive good news that the kingdom of God is here in Jesus.

The kingdom of God is not expanded by armies or laws or police, or any other form of coercion. When the servants of Jesus take up the fight to protect Jesus from Caesar, we end up with crusades, inquisitions, and residential schools. The kingdom of God is not of this world. It is a whole different kind of kingdom that operates on a whole different set of principles.

The cross is not a one-time method that God used as a prelude to his exercise of coercive power to finish the task of our redemption. The cross is God's ongoing strategy, leaving us an example so we should follow in the steps of Jesus, as the apostle Peter wrote.

When the servants of Jesus realize that the kingdom of God is expanded by people willing to sacrifice and even to die, instead of ending up with crusades we end up with Mother Teresa and Dr. Martin Luther King Jr.

As I was working on this chapter I found myself in rush hour on a freeway near my home. Driving in the outside lane, I found myself alongside an empty entry lane that I knew would end just a hundred yards from where my exit lane would begin. As the ramp was empty, I swung out to get ahead of other traffic, knowing I would be off the highway just moments later. I realize this is not the most courteous driving strategy.

A young man driving in front of me apparently shared that realization because, when I pulled out into the empty lane, he pulled halfway out into that lane to block me. Resigned to creep along with everyone else, I pulled back into my lane. The vehicle two cars behind almost immediately had the same thought to avoid traffic, and the guy in front of me made the same response. But the car behind me simply veered further right toward the shoulder, at which time the car in front of me veered further right to block him, leaving the lane in front of me open.

I did not hesitate a moment. I immediately accelerated into his vacated spot and kept my car inches from the truck in front of me so my persecutor could not get back into the lane he had left. Now he had a choice: let me go past him or get caught in the entry lane. I was delighted! He was not. He pulled his car enough in front of me so that I could see him roll down the window to wave at me with one finger.

I was very pleased with myself! But within minutes I was hearing the Holy Spirit whisper a question to me: "Don't you think there is already enough anger in the world? Couldn't you have simply forgiven him for forcing his will on you?"

The way of the cross is not a religious philosophy. It is a way of life: a way of responding to the stresses of daily challenges and the people who cross our paths. Instead of coercing the angry world into a more reasonable behavior, the cross willingly absorbs the anger of the world, knowing that only forgiveness can set us free from a cycle of responsive coercion.

Is that really practical? Didn't the driver who blocked me need to learn a lesson? Wouldn't it have been destructive to my own mental health to simply let it go, to absorb his behavior? (Maybe I should not have tried to get into the entry lane in the first place!)

Seeing the driver's face as he flipped me off, I don't have any question that I was dealing with an angry person. When he arrived home, how did my deepening of his anger influence his interactions with his family? Clearly I don't know. But I would speculate: not positively.

Here's the strange thing. I'm sure we've all been cut off in traffic and been upset at the other driver. But we get over it quickly. It happens, and within minutes, or perhaps even hours, we have forgotten it. But because I responded to aggression with aggression, this incident has mental Velcro. Even as I type this I can feel adrenaline working in my body. It is not only the case that a response of forgiveness on my part would not have made his day worse; it is also the case that my aggressive response actually damaged my own mental health.

To make an observation that seems self-evident: angry responses do not reduce anger. Angry responses increase anger. I was angry because someone I didn't even know was coercing me to drive in a certain way. So, I sought to resolve my anger by coercing him. And we both got angrier. This is the way of empire. If we let it go, we are soon all driving down the freeway in tanks so no one can cut us off!

There are few things as impractical as dying on a cross. How can dying change anything? Don't we need to stand and defend ourselves?

Security seems to be a watchword for today's empires. We must be secure! We worry about financial security. We buy security systems for our homes. We worry about border security. Our fear that we will be victimized is actually much larger than the statistical probability that we will be victimized. Our family life, finances, church policies, politics, educational aspirations, and so much else in life are dedicated to the proposition that we must protect ourselves. We must provide our own security.

Remember, that's how brick walls started. And look where it ends up.

To truly follow Jesus is to know that there are more important matters than our personal safety and security. When that guy pulled out to block me, I was under his power. Had I simply, in the moment, forgiven him, I would have been instantly released from his power. To the degree that I can still feel the adrenaline of the moment just by thinking of it, my own aggression has left me under his power. And I will remain under his power until I can forgive him and let it go.

Jesus exposed himself to danger, arrest, and execution. He did not need to coerce the empire. But the empire needed Jesus to forgive its ignorant violence. The kingdom response to violence is not to buy a gun. It is to live courageously in the face of danger, being willing to suffer for others rather than feeling a constant drive to protect our own safety and security. And, when others have done their worst, to respond: "Father, forgive them. They don't understand what they are doing."

Followers of Jesus will do more than post memes about social justice on Facebook. Followers of Jesus will follow the example of Dutch Christians who wore the Star of David so Nazis could not identify who was actually Jewish. Some of those Dutch Christians died. That is the way of the cross. That is what changes the world.

Followers of Jesus will go to the border and be with those on the other side who are waiting to get in. Followers of Jesus will stand with racial minorities, will be tear-gassed alongside racial minorities, will go to jail with racial minorities. It is through such subversive presence the kingdom of God makes its way into the empire.

The cross is hugely impractical. What difference can a death possibly make?

There is no resurrection unless there is a death. There is no salvation unless someone is willing to break the vicious cycle of coercion, anger, and violence with forgiveness and a willingness to suffer for what it right.

That's why God needed the cross. Not because he was so angry at us. But because we are so angry at us.

6

The Subversive Message
of the New Testament

THE ANCIENT PROCLAMATION WAS given:

> This Gospel is to be proclaimed in every city: Providence
> has granted us and those who will come after us a Saviour
> who has made war to cease and who shall put everything
> in peaceful order. The birthday of our God signalled the
> beginning of Good News for the world because of him.[1]

Who would you think this proclamation describes? Perhaps it
seems already painfully obvious to you, especially when I add the
clue that we continue to celebrate his birthday each year. In fact,
about the same time the above proclamation was read in ancient
cities, a calendar marking the celebration of this person's birth was
inscribed with the words, "We declare the Gospel: The Son of God,
Lord of the world, has come . . . and has brought peace and justice
to the world."

Of course, the Savior Son of God described in these ancient
texts is Caesar Augustus, the Roman emperor at the time Jesus
was born. Every summer we are reminded of his birth throughout

---

1. Ehrenberg and Jones, *Documents Illustrating the Reigns of Augustus and
Tiberius*, 82.

the entire month of August, the month named for him across the empire in 9 BC.

Perhaps you didn't realize we celebrate the birth of a divine emperor. That is how empire works. It just creeps into our lives when we aren't paying close attention.

When I first read this proclamation and other documents written by the emperor's public-relations department, I was struck by how closely these Roman documents borrowed from Christian language. Then I looked at the dates involved. 9 BC. Given these were written before Jesus was even born, clearly it is not the empire that borrowed language from the church, but the church that borrowed language from the empire to describe the meaning of the Messiah: a word meaning "rescuing king" to first-century Jews.

Jesus and his followers were quite aware of these proclamations and often reframed them to explain what God was doing behind the scenes in the world of the empire. For example, when Jesus was asked whether faithful Jews should pay taxes to Caesar, he asked for a coin. Holding it, he questioned, "Whose image is on it?"

At the time, there were still coins in circulation that bore the image of Julius Caesar with an inscription describing him as a divine being. But more common than these coins were coins that bore the image of Augustus Caesar. On the "heads" side that carried Augustus's profile, there was an inscription around the edge that read "Son of God." The "tails" side read "Prince of Peace." Jesus' answer to their question was that, whether they paid taxes or not, his questioners had already capitulated to the idolatry of empire. They had been carrying a declaration of idolatry in their pockets long before the tax bill arrived.

New Testament writers were adept at mocking the empire without seeming to do so. A little knowledge of history will help us understand some of these tongue-in-cheek jokes at the empire's expense. Paul wrote to the Thessalonians, "When they say, 'Peace and Security,' then suddenly destruction comes on them . . . and they will not escape" (1 Thessalonians 5:3 HCSB).

If you were to see a car in many North American cities with the words "To Serve and Protect" painted on the fender, who would you assume that car belongs to? If you're above the speed limit, you slow down right away! You know that is a police car.

The Roman army had a similar slogan: "Peace and Security." That is what Romans genuinely believed their conquests were providing the world. Thessalonica was a regional command center for the Roman military. "Peace and Security" would have been as ubiquitous around Thessalonica as "To Serve and Protect" on the street in front of a police station. This slogan was emblazoned on banners, shields, and perhaps even the fenders of their chariots.

In that light we read again what Paul wrote to the Christians in this military city: "When they say, 'Peace and Security,' then suddenly destruction comes . . . and they will not escape." The Roman army only brought peace and security to Romans. If you were a citizen of a region the Romans wanted to add to the empire, as soon as you saw banners headed toward your border reading "Peace and Security," you could be certain your own near future would involve sudden destruction.

Paul was clearly implying his readers should not trust the empire to provide peace and security, even though Romans were convinced their culture and law would bring those benefits. (If you find it difficult to believe people could be so self-deluded, consider how often legally elected governments have been undermined and overthrown in the name of protecting democracy.)

Paul delivers this warning in a passage about the coming of Jesus. The Greek word he often uses to describe this is *parousia*. The Romans used the same word when, after they had conquered a city, they made a public announcement to the populace that they had come to bring peace and justice. Paul wrote that we wait for a coming of a different king to bring peace and security to us.

Many readers consider the apostle Paul to be a "law and or-der" kind of guy. It is impossible to have a debate about Christians and civil disobedience without someone quoting Paul's letter to the Romans, "Let every person be subject to the governing authorities, for there is no authority except from God, and those that exist are instituted by God" (Romans 13:1).

A former attorney general of the United States used this text to justify inhumane treatment of migrants at his nation's southern border. Had he realized the deeply subversive argument Paul was making to the church at Rome, the heart of the empire, the attorney general would never have used this verse except to imply the government was overstepping its legitimate use of authority.

Some of the first recipients of this letter to the church in Rome were Roman citizens, greatly benefiting by their connection to the empire. Others of these first recipients were slaves who had been stolen from their homes and brought against their will to serve Roman masters. Obviously, this group had little reason to love and respect their Roman owners. Each of these groups would read or hear this letter a little differently. But all of them were familiar with the language of the empire. The slogans and clichés of the empire surrounded them.

Let's see if we can read this letter as it would have struck these diverse people living in Rome two thousand years ago. They would have grown up hearing about and being taught the gospel. That is, the gospel of Augustus Caesar, Son of God, the Divine Julius, and Lord of the world. The gospel was the way Augustus had brought peace and justice to the entire world. Some had learned this at the knee of their parents, others from their masters. And now they had a letter that begins:

> Paul, a servant of Christ Jesus, called to be an apostle, set apart for the gospel of God, which he promised beforehand through his prophets in the holy Scriptures, concerning his Son, who was descended from David according to the flesh and was declared to be the Son of God in power according to the Spirit of holiness by his resurrection from the dead, Jesus Christ our Lord, through whom we have received grace and apostleship to bring about the obedience of faith for the sake of his name among all the nations, including you who are called to belong to Jesus Christ . . . (Romans 1:1–6)

To first-century Roman ears, this would sound both familiar and different. It was what they had been taught all along, but in a twisted sort of way. They were still hearing gospel about a Divine Son. But instead of Augustus, descended from the Divine Julius Caesar, this was a king descended from David, historical king of a small, obscure nation that had been since conquered by a string of empires and now was under the full control of Rome. What kind of caesar was that!?

It became more bizarre. The proof that this new Son of the Divine was deity himself had nothing to do with conquering the world and protecting his subjects. His deity was confirmed by conquering death in an incredible story about being executed by the empire and then experiencing resurrection from the dead.

And now, the letter's writer continues, this new divine king was requiring "the obedience of faith" among "all the nations, including you!" Who are the "you" in this statement? Romans! Rulers of the known world! Citizens of the most powerful empire who, just for the record, have conquered the obscure nation from which this king comes. Romans had demonstrated the extent of their power over this proposed divine Son of God by executing him in the cruel and humiliating fashion reserved for dissidents and slaves.

How would this have sounded to Roman ears? This would have made no sense at all!

As Paul continues to elaborate on this good news for all nations, he begins with some pretty bad news. "The wrath of God is revealed from heaven against all . .,. who by their unrighteousness suppress the truth" (Romans 1:18). Paul then describes this suppression of truth as "exchang[ing] the glory of the immortal God for images resembling mortal man and birds and animals and creeping things" (Romans 1:23). That is, replacing the glory of God as he really is by attributing divine glory to human beings, such as Augustus, or Julius Caesar, for example.

The letter goes on to describe how God is going to restore the entire universe to the way it ought to be. This will include restoring all nations, Jewish and Gentile alike, to the way they really ought to be. The Romans and their empire are among those things requiring change and restoration. In the city where this letter was to be read publicly among the church, this was seditious, if not outright treasonous. Reading this aloud in public was asking to be arrested and possibly killed.

And that's okay! Because according to this gospel of the Divine Son, the universe and all nations will not become what they should be through the force of the empire's army or through Caesar Augustus. The nations will only be remedied by Jesus, who rescues us from the effects of making gods out of things and people who aren't really God. His remedy includes a cross.

To restore the world so that it is right and good requires that God dismantle all of our tribal idolatries. In such a world there is no nation that is exceptional because of its special relationship with God, including even the Jewish nation or the Roman Empire centered in the city to which this letter was directed.

Until this restoration is achieved, Paul maintains that there is a legitimate place for Caesar and his government: "[Caesar] is God's servant for your good. But if you do wrong, be afraid, for he does not bear the sword in vain. For he is the servant of God" (Romans 13:4). This offers an important clarification. Caesar does not rule because he is a god. Caesar is able to govern because God rules.

As long as Caesar is exercising human authority for the common good, he deserves four things: taxes, tolls, respect, and honor. Paul is not proposing that Caesar be overthrown or eliminated. But Paul is definitely demoting him! Caesar exists only to be a servant of God and a servant of the people for God's sake. This was not the prevailing ideology in Rome!

Furthermore, Paul was convinced Caesar was merely a temporary arrangement until the real King, the real Son of God, arrives on the scene. It is only the *parousia* of Christ that will accomplish peace and justice. All of this is a reversal of the language used by the empire describing Augustus ascending to his throne. When Jesus comes, Augustus will bend the knee to Jesus, just as other kings and rulers bent the knee to Caesar when he appeared as a gesture of their willingness to submit to his greater authority.

At the end of things, the real king is not Augustus.

> It is said,
> "Rejoice, O Gentiles, with his people."
> And again,
> "Praise the Lord, all you Gentiles,
> and let all the peoples extol him."
> And again Isaiah says,
> "The root of Jesse will come,
> even he who arises to rule the Gentiles;
> in him will the Gentiles hope." (Romans 15:1–12)

Even citizens of the powerful Roman empire have cause to hope in the Jewish king who will arise to rule the Gentiles. Paul insists that this is not a threat to Rome, but a reason for joy and celebration. But it means that Caesar's power and authority are limited in both scope and time.

We should read this understanding that Paul and his Christian readers were fully convinced that the *parousia* of Christ "who arises to rule the Gentiles" was imminent. Tomorrow, if not today. Augustus himself would still be alive to see the day every knee should bow at the name of Jesus (Philippians 2:10). The time most of his world would spend under Caesar's thumb was so short it should be of little concern. The empire's days were numbered.

For the slaves and vanquished of Rome, the imminent coming of Jesus was not simply religious vindication; it was political liberation.

Notwithstanding all that I have written thus far, it is nevertheless the case that Paul was more than willing to make use of the various tools the empire provided to assist him in carrying the message of the coming King around the Roman world. Paul himself was a citizen of Rome. It is unclear how Paul's family acquired Roman citizenship, but Paul claimed he was born a citizen. This afforded him certain rights, such as the right to a trial before being executed. His citizenship helped Paul evade a lynch mob at least once.

Paul's call to be apostle to the Gentiles while others reached the Jews would have been strengthened by his citizenship. It would have enhanced his status in Gentile eyes. On the other hand, some scholars have suggested that one of many points of contention between Paul and the Hebrew believers was precisely this citizenship. As a Roman citizen, Paul may well have been regarded by them as less Jewish. This would be a charge his close relationship with many Gentiles would have seemed to verify.

Citizenship may have been a two-edged sword for Paul. But he used it for the cause of the gospel, and there were times it was quite helpful to be able to claim it.

While Paul mocked the peace and security the empire claimed to bring, he also made extensive use of Pax Romana, the order and infrastructure Rome brought that allowed for relatively safe travel and communication around the empire. The rapid spread of Christianity across the empire cannot be understood apart from Pax Romana. There were ways the empire was, undeniably, useful to Paul.

While Paul was willing to make use of benefits provided by Rome, he was on guard against its values and beliefs. He understood that empire and idolatry always end up blurring into a symbiotic worldview. Paul did not place his faith at the service of the empire to undergird imperial authorities. But he was opportunistic about using the empire's resources and infrastructure to proclaim as widely as possible a message that challenged the empire. A better king had come and was coming to replace the current system.

While Paul used his citizenship to his advantage, he regarded it not only as temporary but as something of a spiritual fiction. Every nationality was absorbed into Christ. Twice in his letters to churches Paul eliminates any distinction between Jew, Greek, barbarian, and Scythian; slave or free; male or female, "but Christ is all, and in all" (Colossians 3:11). This inclusiveness also works the other way around: "you are all one in Christ" (Galatians 3:28).

Empire and nationalism require a division of humanity between us and them. Paul rejects all of those divisions as artificial, human constructs that no longer have meaning or significance in Christ. In the present, temporary order of things, they may offer some convenience, but they really should not be taken too seriously.

In the alternative community of the church, to recognize and enshrine artificial distinctions between us and them is not only irrelevant; it is destructive and dangerous. We see this in Paul's instructions to the Corinthians related to the Lord's Supper. Most churchgoers are familiar with the warning: "Whoever, therefore, eats the bread or drinks the cup of the Lord in an unworthy manner . . . without discerning the body eats and drinks judgment on himself" (1 Corinthians 11:17, 29).

This warning is generally taken to refer to participating in the Lord's Table without truly believing it or fully understanding it. Others warn against eating while having unconfessed sin or unresolved conflict. But these explanations neglect the context of the warning.

What we now generally observe as the Lord's Supper or the Eucharist was part of a larger meal in the first-century church in Corinth. To understand Paul's concern, we have to know how a dinner party was shared at the time. Someone with a house large enough to host a large dinner party would have a central dining area with other rooms leading off it. The most prestigious guests—generally the most wealthy—would eat in the central room. Each of the other rooms would represent steps down the social ladder, each lower than the previous room until they came to the most menial slaves.

As each part of the meal was served, it would first come to the central room. Only when the most highly honored guests had completed their course would that food be taken to those in the next room, while people further down the pecking order continued to wait. As this progressed from room to room, the best of the food was taken. By the time the chicken got to the final dining area, the breasts were long gone. All that was left were necks and backs. This is what Paul was describing: "In eating, each one goes ahead with his own meal. One goes hungry and another gets drunk" (1 Corinthians 11:21).

A chapter earlier, while describing the liturgical meaning of the bread and cup, Paul had written, "Because there is one bread, we who are many are one body, for we all partake of the one bread" (10:17). By following their custom of segregating socio-economic classes in their practice of the Lord's Supper, the Corinthians were not discerning the body. They were denying the basic oneness of rich and poor, slave and free. For "humiliating the those who have nothing" Paul indicted them: "You despise the church of God" (11:22).

This line of thought took a more radical turn when Paul sent a runaway slave back to his owner, Philemon, with a letter. Paul simply requested that Philemon welcome Onesimus home "no longer as a slave but more than a slave, a beloved brother" (Philemon 16). The gospel of Jesus has trumped the social order. For Philemon and Onesimus this was much more than a theoretical recognition of equality before God; this had real monetary and life-changing consequences. The differences that had divided them into separate classes of people had been overwhelmed by their fundamental oneness in Christ.

When Paul described the evaporation of human distinctions in Christ, he was not merely offering a nice thought. He was upsetting the social and political applecart. While he was happy to claim Roman citizenship when it was helpful, it was not, for Paul, actual reality. Paul believed it essential that, regardless their diverse national, cultural, and religious backgrounds, those following Jesus could no longer think of other people as "strangers and aliens, but you are fellow citizens with the saints and members of the household of God" (Ephesians 2:19).

Just as Israel was called to be an alternative to the empire of Egypt and its values, the church continues to be called to become an alternative community to today's political and economic empires. In Christ there cannot be rich and poor, American and Mexican, male and female. We are one. We belong to each other. If some of us have more resources than others, "your abundance at the present time should supply their need, so that their abundance may supply your need, that there may be fairness" (2 Corinthians 8:14).

Paul lived in an empire. But the empire did not live in Paul. His values and relationships were formed by the nature of the kingdom of God. The church later became indistinguishable from the empire. But it was not meant to be so.

In this world of large political and economic circles of influence gathered around nations and corporations, there are possibilities for communicating, training, and organizing the people of God that have been developed by our empires. Making use of these tools for the spread of an alternative set of values and beliefs is fine. But the church's values and beliefs must be a distinct alternative to the ultimately deadening effects of empire.

Local gatherings of the church are not businesses in competition with one another, but you would be hard-pressed to discern that from church advertising or congregational websites. Pastors are not CEOs with a mandate to expand their church's and their personal brand to gather a larger and larger share of the market. But you would not know this from reading the vast majority of books and articles written about the contemporary practice of ministry.

Measuring an effective church requires a completely different metric from measuring an effective business. The measurement is not the money or people gathered into the church. The measurement is the positive impact the church has on the world around it.

The measurement is also the degree of diversity, equality, and inclusiveness expressed by people in the church. A monoracial church in a multiracial community is a contradiction in terms. A monogenerational church in a multigenerational community is equally a contradiction in terms. Perhaps the best way to get a number of white eighteen- to thirty-five-year-olds into the church is to create a church that caters so much to that demographic that few people outside that demographic come. The problem is, that's not getting those people into a church. The number that gather in such a community is irrelevant, because such a community is failing to discern the body of Christ in people of other races and ages. It is an organization growing by empire values, tools, and standards. This organization may genuinely believe it is following and believing in Jesus, but when compared to the actual teaching and example of Jesus, a significant gap of belief is revealed.

There is a tension here. This is the great difficulty of living for the kingdom while also living at the empire's heart. Tools of the empire will aid our kingdom work. But it is natural and easy for an empire worldview to enter the church with those tools. The empire offers strategies that will maximize the popular appeal of the church to our Roman neighbors. Those strategies might themselves be built on values contrary to the kingdom.

The church-growth movement, for example, sought to multiply followers of Jesus by organizing churches according to the "homogenous unit principle": that is, collecting people who are similar to one another because people are most comfortable joining groups of people like themselves. That might be good for increasing numbers of people converting to belief in Christ. But it is only a very short-term good. In the longer term, it fails the world, the church, and the individual believer by failing to create community across racial and socioeconomic barriers.

To measure a strategy by its success in increasing the number of people and financial resources available is to return to the underlying principles of empire: acquisition and protection of "our" position. A kingdom strategy is more likely to measure success by how it brings people together. And this not only in the church but by impact on the wider community, bringing diverse people together as friends and neighbors.

7

An Ancient Gallery of Modern Art

PABLO PICASSO WAS A fascinating artist. While still a boy he replicated the work of masters. As his painting matured he began to display an increasing amount of expressiveness in his work. His well-known painting *The Guitar Player*, for example, records the guitarist's body with general physiological accuracy. But the color selections and flow of shapes that make up the man and guitar convey a mood more than the merely accurate rendering of an old man playing guitar possibly could.

Picasso was trying to depict reality in a way photographs cannot. As he became increasingly abstract, many people didn't (and don't) know what to make of his work.

According to one story, Picasso was once waiting on a train platform when a man approached him to ask, "Are you Picasso, the painter?"

"I am."

"Can you explain to me why you don't paint things the way they actually appear?"

Picasso replied that he did not understand the question. Reaching into his wallet, the man produced a photo of his wife.

"Look," he said, "This is what my wife actually looks like. But my guess is you would paint her with both eyes on one side of her head!"

Picasso reached out for the photo. Examining the black-and-white surface, he asked, "Is this really what she looks like? She's very pale and quite small for an adult," and turning the photo to look at an edge he continued, "And she's dangerously thin!"

Paintings by Picasso and other modern artists take time to absorb. They have to be felt as much as they are seen. To "get them" we can't simply glance at them, identify what they represent, and move to the next piece along the wall. Such art does more than describe a scene. It evokes a set of feelings and questions. To try to read these paintings literally is to provoke frustration while missing the point.

If we're trying to read and understand Revelation, the final book of the Bible, it helps if we have an appreciation for artists such as Picasso. Like a gallery full of modern art, Revelation presents us with a series of images that do not describe reality with a literal paintbrush. These images are designed to evoke emotional and spiritual reactions in those viewing the work. To attempt reading Revelation literally simply provokes frustration while missing the point.

Revelation does not stand alone as an isolated piece of literature. It is one example of a Jewish literary form developed during the time the Jewish people were being oppressed by the Babylonian Empire, about six hundred years before Revelation was written. Many examples of this writing style have been preserved. They are full of images filled with symbolic meaning, much of that meaning being derived from the emotional tone of the images.

This Jewish literary form is called apocalyptic literature. The etymological root of the word *apocalyptic* is "to pull aside," like opening the curtains or unrolling a scroll. Apocalyptic literature aims to uncover the truth but must be read by looking beneath or through the writer's word pictures. It is not meant to be taken literally.

There is a reason apocalyptic literature was developed during an experience of foreign oppression. The spirituals sung by

American slaves were a coded way of conveying messages slave masters could not understand. Likewise, this Jewish literature was a way of critiquing sinful empires and describing God's ultimate victory over them. The Jewish people did not separate the religious and the political into distinct categories. Political commentary was spiritual observation, and spiritual observation led to political conclusions. In periods of oppression, such commentary and observation required symbolism as an important protection against imprisonment or execution.

The last book of the Bible was written by John, most probably the apostle. John was writing from the island of Patmos. For years I had a mental image of John living lazy days as an old man on a small Greek island. I imagined Roman authorities had contained him on an island to isolate him, limiting his contact and influence. But, I reasoned, if you have to be in isolation at all, an Aegean island would not be the worst place to suffer such a fate.

In fact, Patmos was a prison island because it was home to a major rock quarry. John spent his days with the other prisoners doing slave labor, breaking and shaping stones for Roman use. John was not spending his days on a patio overlooking the sea sipping his morning espresso, then strolling down to the post office to drop his latest epistle in the mail. Patmos was a hard, dangerous place.

If John wanted to get his writing past prison censors, he had to be careful. Were he to write directly: "This evil Roman Empire is doomed to defeat! The God of Jesus and the Jews will have victory over Rome!" imagine the response. His guards would not only have destroyed the letter. John would have soon found himself breaking bigger rocks with a smaller hammer.

So John did what the Jewish people like him had done for centuries. He wrote in symbols and images that would only have meaning to Jewish readers already familiar with apocalyptic literature. This is not a modern document with logically arranged ideas. It is a gallery of emotive images belonging to the ancient world.

The book of Revelation contains seven visions. There is an order to these seven visions. They each describe political and social events happening in the world as John wrote. But these events have always been happening in the world and always will happen until Jesus comes again. The purpose of Revelation is not to give literal descriptions of specific incidents and people that will appear at the very end of history. That is a fairly modern reading of the book that does not take into account the study of first-century Jewish literature available to us.

To read Revelation well, we have to imagine we are ancient people with an ancient view of the world who happen to have stumbled into a museum of modern art. I realize this is no small feat. Some moderns will not be comfortable with the powerful images of an evil spiritual being called Satan. Others may not be comfortable abandoning the effort to read these words literally. Either of these discomforts will get in the way of properly allowing us to understand this strange book of the Bible. To get it we have to just go with it.

The visions were written for followers of Jesus who were undergoing increasing persecution from the Roman Empire. Like churches everywhere, they had their own share of internal problems and conflicts to deal with as well. Each vision observes the same kind of interactions between God, his people, and human authorities and empires. Each vision tries to understand not merely what is happening, but *why* it is happening. What they mean. Who is behind them.

The first vision begins with several personal and localized events happening in seven churches near the island of Patmos. Each of these churches is facing its own pain, conflict, temptation, and external pressure. As the visions progress, that localized scope of suffering is enlarged to include the entire world. The church suffers because it is located in a world that suffers. We are part of a bigger ecosystem.

The progressing visions also increase in depth. The horrible things that happen in the world are revealed to be, in fact, an intense spiritual conflict that expresses itself on a human stage. Good and evil are at war. God and Satan are in a colossal battle. Sometimes it seems as if evil and Satan are winning. But each vision ends with a notice that God is unfolding his plan, and the victory of good over evil, God over Satan, is certain.

The fourth vision (recorded in chapters 12 and 13) begins with a woman, a dragon, and a baby. The woman is "clothed with the sun, with the moon under feet, and on her head a crown of twelve stars" (Revelation 12:1). Numbers are important identifiers in apocalyptic literature. There were twelve tribes of Israel, twelve disciples of Jesus: the woman represents the people of God.

The dragon doesn't require much of a clue. John outright identifies it in verse 18 as "that ancient serpent, who is called the devil and Satan, the deceiver of the whole world."

The woman gives birth to a baby, "a male child, one who is to rule all the nations." We find the dragon waiting and ready to devour the baby immediately upon birth. But just as the dragon is ready to pounce, the baby is snatched away by God.

Remembering some of the details surrounding the birth and death of Jesus, this image recalls two events at the beginning and end of his life. When Jesus was born in Bethlehem, King Herod, who ruled as the Romans' lackey, sent soldiers to destroy every boy under the age of two in the small town. But, in a dream, an angel warned Joseph to flee, and Jesus was snatched away before the soldiers could kill him.

Again, at the end of his story, it looked as if Satan had snuffed the life out of Jesus. Imprisoned in the grave, there seemed no further life for the movement of his followers. Just when it all seemed under the dragon's control, Jesus was snatched from the grave to heaven and his Father's side.

But the woman, the people of God, was still on earth. Unable to assault Jesus, in the vision the dragon turns its attention to the people of God to destroy the woman. This is why life is not easy for the people of God. But as we read through the vision, each time it looks as if the dragon finally has the woman cornered and is ready to destroy her, God comes to her rescue. Each time this happens, the dragon becomes more furious with the woman and tries all the harder to destroy her.

Over many generations and in many times and places the dragon has tried to destroy God's people. But never with complete success.

Here is where the vision gets interesting to a discussion about human empires. Because Satan is unable to destroy the people of God, he recruits two allies to his cause. The first is "a beast rising out of the sea, with ten horns and seven heads, with ten diadems on its horns and blasphemous names on its heads" (Revelation 13:1). Remember, we're looking at a picture designed to elicit an emotive response from us. Thinking like an ancient person visiting a museum of modern art, how do you respond to this image?

As the image continues, Jewish believers reared with the apocalyptic literature that had been floating around their culture for six hundred years would have quickly recognized this beast to represent civic or imperial government. The beast out of the sea has power to wage war. Further, this beast has authority over tribes, peoples, and nations.

This beast is not necessarily a specific empire, throne, or government. It represents an assortment of governments that have been scattered through time around the world. Did you notice earlier a discrepancy between the heads and the horns? There are ten horns, but seven heads, each horn bearing a crown.

In this literature seven is a good number: the number of God. The notion of government is not a bad notion. In fact, the notion of government begins with God. The dragon, however, has made a career out of taking good gifts God has given humanity and twisting them toward its own destructive purposes.

Meanwhile, the number ten represented the Roman Empire, which loved to use groupings of ten as an organizing principle. But the Roman Empire is long gone.

One interesting feature of this beast's crowned horns is that when a head is mortally wounded its wound manages to heal itself. There has been an inevitable cycle to history: when one repressive, empire-building government falls, another simply arises to take its place. At times the world has witnessed the end of an evil empire and celebrated, "This is finally over!" But it never is. Kingdoms fall. Kingdoms rise. As those who live within an empire, when the kingdom of our enemies falls and the Berlin Wall comes down, we rejoice. But as the empire begins to rise elsewhere we are filled with anxiety and fear. The Tower of Babel repeats itself as our insecurity drives us to redivide the world into "them" and "us."

John is making it quite clear that the empire (the beast rising out of the sea) is allied with the devil (the red dragon). It is a subservient relationship. The beast may not realize this, but underlying the human tools of empire is a demonic presence of evil.

And it is not only the Roman Empire John sees aligned with Satan. Nor is it some particular political leader in the future, right before the end of the world, that is going to fill the role of this beast. A succession of empires throughout history has been inspired by Satan to destroy the work and people of God in the world. Empire is not just a bad human idea. According to Revelation, it is the civic embodiment of evil.

This might seem an unduly harsh assessment, given that some empires have been friendly to Christianity. This objection brings us to the dragon's second ally in its mission to destroy the people of God.

> Then I saw another beast rising out of the earth. It had two horns like a lamb and it spoke like a dragon. It exercises all the authority of the first beast in its presence, and makes the earth and its inhabitants worship the first beast, whose mortal wound was healed. It performs great signs, even making fire come down from heaven to earth in front of people. (Revelation 13:11–13)

This second "beast rising out of the earth" is a religious ally of the dragon. It might look like a lamb. But it sounds like a dragon. It works miracles and directs people to worship. The second beast leaves its mark on people: on their heads and how they think, and on their hands and how they act.

When heavy-metal music was at its peak, it was not uncommon to see young white guys in black T-shirts emblazoned with big Gothic numerals: 666. They imagined this made a dark statement about themselves: "I'm bad! I am the seed of the devil!"

In fact, 666 is not a reference to the devil. The number by which this religious beast is known is "the number of man [humanity] and his number is 666" (Revelation 13:18). The original readers of John's vision knew that seven was a holy number because God rested on the seventh day. Humanity was created on the sixth day, making six the number of humanity. The worst those poor guys in the black T-shirts were actually saying was, "Yeah, I'm a humanist."

Devil worship is not the object of the religious beast. The religious beast simply wants to draw our focus from God as he is to a smaller god who serves and undergirds the empire. Rather than drawing attention to what God is doing, the beast focuses on things humans do through the agency of government and empire. In this arrangement, empire religion draws its power from the political empire while ascribing divine authority to that empire in return. The religious beast may well declare itself to be building the kingdom of God, but this religion does so in ways that leave God, his character, and his values out of it. It looks like a lamb. But it sounds like a dragon.

A brief walk through history easily demonstrates how the beast of government and the beast of religion work together, whether the religion is Christian or something else (including state atheism). At the time John wrote Revelation, the official religion of the Roman Empire included Caesar worship. There was a reason the Romans hated the Jews and then the Christians as much as they did. In all the empire, these were the only two monotheistic religious communities. Polytheistic faiths were able to simply add Caesar to their existing pantheons of deities. But Jews and Christians believed that to worship Caesar was to renounce the God in whom they believed. To Rome, this was treason.

For several generations Rome tried to destroy the woman: the people of God. The beast of political and military power accompanied by the beast of state religion tried again and again to eradicate the church of Jesus without success.

This strategy came to an end in AD 313 when Emperor Constantine converted to Christianity. Whether his conversion was sincere has been debated. Whether religiously genuine or not, it was a brilliant political move. If it was not possible to absorb Christians into the culture and values of the empire using Roman religion as a unifying principle, why not make use of this new and growing faith as the unifying principle of the empire?

Virtually overnight persecution of Christians stopped. Christianity itself became the state religion. The church became wealthy and politically powerful. For a millennium and a half, the Christian church became entwined with the governments of Europe. The line of demarcation between spiritual authority and political power became blurred to the point of invisibility.

With the empire's wealth and power, the church no longer felt it needed God. At no point in its history has the church gained political power without a corresponding loss of spiritual power and life. As Jesus said, we can serve either God or Mammon (wealth and all its trappings, including power). We cannot serve both. What several centuries of direct persecution could not do, Rome finally accomplished by co-opting the church into the values and culture of the empire. The danger of a God who hears the groans of the oppressed was tamed.

Remember that the beast from the earth inserts humanity into the place that rightly belongs to God. Again, a survey of history quickly reveals the spiritual cost of this. When the church attaches itself to a particular government and its levers of power, inevitably that church turns to coercion as a way of bringing people under God's sway. Even violence becomes a means of evangelism.

One does not have to look hard at more recent history to see plenty of examples. The continent on which I live was colonized (a defining mark of empire) by European Christians who slaughtered the original inhabitants of the Americas and then isolated the defeated survivors into ever-shrinking reservations. The final insult is to then claim, "This country is built on the foundation of Judeo-Christian values!"

One of the most shocking and depressing examples of the dragon's two allies working together happened in my own country. Church and state came together to create residential schools so indigenous children could be taught and enculturated into the "superior" Christian culture brought by white Europeans. This arrogance resulted in years of physical and sexual abuse of children by Christian clergy.

This is demonic. Which is exactly the point this vision makes. It is important to realize that John is not saying this begins with a pope or a king, a pastor or a president. John is showing us that the marriage of religion and government is a strategy of the devil himself. Put another way, the dragon was unable to destroy the people of God. But if the dragon could get these two beasts working together, the alignment of political power and religion always destroys the church by eroding its spiritual power from within.

Just as Paul warned that when the Thessalonians saw banners promising "Peace and Security" they needed to be on guard, John warns us that when we see Christian leaders describing political figures and parties as "the Christian candidate, God's person for the time," we need to beware. Otherwise the values of our Lord and Savior will give way to the expedience and coercion of human politics and violence.

8

More from the Revelation Gallery

HAVE YOU EVER NOTICED how much advertising assumes we are stupid? How likely are you to walk out to your driveway, climb into a fun car, and instead of your usual commute to work suddenly find yourself cruising along a winding California highway over-looking the ocean? Are auto advertisers suggesting the allure of a new car will cause us to skip work to go for a nice drive? I doubt that is the intent of the commercial. After all, if we skip work, how are we are going to make those payments for the next five years?

Or perhaps they are suggesting their racy sports car will simply be so much fun our usual commute will feel like a winding Californian highway. As it happens, I have driven to work through bumper-to-bumper traffic in a fun little sports car. My rush-hour freeway drive did not feel like a winding highway. You might ask, did I buy into the ad? What can I say? They do it because it works. Even when we think we know better.

This chapter will carry us further into the ancient modern art gallery known as the book of Revelation. The images we find in this room help us understand the relationship between the ads that engage our desires and the world of empire.

The sixth apocalyptic vision of John paints portraits of two women, each of whom is attractive in her own way. One is a sweet girl. She is pure and innocent: the kind of girl a young man would be happy to take home to meet his mother.

A healthy young man might find the other attractive, too. But it is a certainty Mom is not going to like her at all. She wears too much makeup and too little of anything else. She is the infamous whore of Babylon.

If I were speaking to you face to face, I might be concerned about calling her by her real name, fearing it would embarrass you. And embarrassing you would embarrass me. So it is tempting to simply call her the bad girl of Babylon. But that jolt of discomfort, that sour flavor of bad taste in polite company, is exactly what her name is meant to evoke in us. We are fascinated and horrified to find such a person in our circle.

The whore of Babylon is a woman of low morals with friends in high places. The kings of the earth have enjoyed her bed (Revelation 17:2). She is very wealthy. She dresses herself in the most expensive fashion and jewelry. As it turns out, the devil does sometimes wear Prada. Or, at least, his friends do. Forget a silver spoon. She drinks from a golden cup.

Perhaps the easiest way to understand what this rich prostitute represents is to observe who will grieve her loss when she is finally gone.

> And the merchants of the earth weep and mourn for her, since no one buys their cargo anymore, cargo of gold, silver, jewels, pearls, fine linen, purple cloth, silk, scarlet cloth, all kinds of scented wood, all kinds of articles of ivory, all kinds of articles of costly wood, bronze, iron and marble, cinnamon, spice, incense, myrrh, frankincense, wine, oil, fine flour, wheat, cattle and sheep, horses and chariots, and slaves, that is, human souls . . . .
> And all shipmasters and seafaring men, sailors and all whose trade is on the sea, stood far off and cried out as they saw the smoke of her burning,
> "Alas, alas, for the great city
> where all who had ships at sea
> grew rich by her wealth!
> For in a single hour she has been laid waste." (Revelation 18:11–13, 17–19)

The whore of Babylon represents the manufacture, collection, and exchange of wealth and goods. We might call her our system of commerce. She is not just one business and certainly not just one businessperson. Not every company or businessperson is necessarily part of the whore of Babylon. But it requires care and integrity to avoid her.

To whatever degree we participate in business in a manner that traffics in human souls, however, we are part of this bad girl. She is unafraid to leave widows homeless. She considers the poor a product of their own lack of intelligence and ambition. She certainly doesn't feel any compulsion to help them from the resources of her own wealth.

And she is closely related to the concept of empire. In fact, she is mounted on the beast with seven heads and ten horns that we saw in the last room we visited in the gallery: the beast of government.

> This calls for a mind with wisdom: the seven heads are seven mountains on which the woman is seated; they are also seven kings, five of whom have fallen, one is, the other has not yet come, and when he does come he must remain only a little while. As for the beast that was and is not, it is an eighth but it belongs to the seven, and it goes to destruction. And the ten horns that you saw are ten kings who have not yet received royal power, but they are to receive authority as kings for one hour, together with the beast. (Revelation 17:8–12)

This is actually not as complicated as it first appears. There are seven kings, five have fallen; one is; and one is still to come. In the history of the Bible, as of the time John wrote Revelation, six different empires had conquered and oppressed God's people: Egypt, Assyria, Babylon, Persia, and Greece had already risen and fallen. The sixth of these empires, Rome, was still in power. But John predicted the Roman Empire would not last forever. It, too, would eventually fall and be replaced by yet another empire.

Not only did these empires cause difficulty for God's people, but there were many other nations or kings that had gone to war with the Jews to take their land or their goods. These were all governments that existed for a time and then were gone. This is the cycle of governments, nations, empires, and powers. They arise for a time. Then they fall.

The point of this sequence of kingdoms is not to give us a literal baseline so we can count the empires and powerful nations to figure out exactly where we are on a timeline for Jesus to return. As Jesus said, "Nation will rise against nation, and kingdom against kingdom . . . All these are but the beginning of the birth pains" (Matthew 24:7–8).

The important element of this picture is that it doesn't matter which empire is in power; the whore of Babylon, the systems and infrastructure of commerce, ride them all, surviving each falling empire. The whore will ride whatever government brings her the most wealth at any point in time. She doesn't care whether the beast of the day is communist or fascist. She doesn't care whether the beast of the day is a democracy or a dictatorship. All she cares about is her profit margin.

It is an odd relationship between the beast and the whore, government and commerce. The whore provides the beast with much it needs. If the beast of the day is a dictatorship, the whore will sell it arms. If the beast of the day is a democracy, the whore will donate to the campaign and produce compelling advertisements to keep the beast in power. She has a way to lure all of them into her bed. The beast needs her wealth.

But the relationship won't last forever. Eventually the beast comes to hate the whore (Revelation 17:16). At some point the beast will eventually recognize that the whore has sucked everything dry and will turn on her. This often happens at the point that so much wealth is going to the whore that the empire can no longer sustain its expansion. The empire begins to implode and crumble from within. The emperor thought he was in power, but it was the system of commerce that was tugging the reins the whole time.

The whore doesn't mind. She knows someone else will want to make use of her wealth and she will have a new beast to ride very soon.

Like the other images in Revelation, it is not hard to look around the twenty-first-century world we live in and observe the continuation of the weird relationship between commerce and government. In rich and poor nations alike, governments always need money. Commerce always needs markets. This is not rocket science.

Consequently, governments open their doors and borders to business. Economic prosperity is one of the major measuring sticks people use when evaluating the quality of their political leaders. Business rides that public need.

Sooner or later, though, government or the public or both notice that a disproportionate amount of the wealth business is generating is going to only a very few people. When the connection between commerce and government operates for the benefit of all people, the relationship goes well. The whore of Babylon has only taken over when the main principle that drives the relationship between business and commerce is keeping a handful of people wealthy and powerful. Those very few people can deflect attention from this by pointing to some other group that is taking work and wealth from the multitude who keep the few in power.

Eventually, even this distraction stops working, and government and public alike turn against the systems of commerce to bring them under control. But it's not long until whatever new structures have been put into place are following the same systems and using the same infrastructures that have always belonged to the whore of Babylon.

At the time John wrote Revelation, the whole structure of the Roman Empire existed to suck wealth out of its colonies and carry it back to Rome. Today multinational corporations follow the same principle on a global scale. Today's empires are more driven by corporate activity than ever before. Militarily we have reached the point that using our most powerful weapons will destroy everyone. In our world the military form of empire is increasingly replaced by economic empires.

The whore of Babylon makes her decisions by only one criterion: Does it profit me? Is it expedient? God watches and asks a different question: Is it moral? Is it good for all my creation?

What does it mean that God will judge the world? God's judgment is not about anger, punishment, or retribution. As James wrote, "Mercy triumphs over judgment" (James 2:13).

God is always working to restore creation to his original intent and design. The New Testament does not anticipate going back to the garden of Eden so much as going forward to a holy city where people live in harmony, joy, and close connection to God and each other. This holy city resonates with the healing of all nations.

This future joy toward which Christians hope is a future designed for what God will bring into our eternity. God watches and judges how we live with each other. God will only bring into eternity what is good. As God breaks into the interaction of political power and economic wealth, the whore of Babylon, the imperial systems and infrastructure of commerce, will of necessity be eliminated.

> So will Babylon the great city be thrown down with violence,
>> and will be found no more;
> and the sound of harpists and musicians, of flute players and
>> trumpeters,
>> will be heard in you no more,
> and a craftsman of any craft
>> will be found in you no more,
> and the sound of the mill
>> will be heard in you no more,
> and the light of a lamp
>> will shine in you no more,
> and the voice of bridegroom and bride
>> will be heard in you no more,
> for your merchants were the great ones of the earth,
>> and all nations were deceived by your sorcery.
> And in her was found the blood of prophets and of saints,
>> and of all who have been slain on earth.
>> (Revelation 18:21–24)

This is such a sad picture. Imagine a city without music. Perhaps the saddest is the picture of a city in which the voice of bridegroom and bride are no longer heard. This is obviously not the holy city toward which God is moving us.

Nevertheless, there is a place in which the voice of bridegroom and bride are heard and celebrated. A huge wedding feast is about to begin! While I offer no textual evidence for this, I'm pretty sure there is going to be a pretty amazing band. What a wonderful opportunity for Christians who have been afraid to dance to finally learn how!

> Then I heard what seemed to be the voice of a great multitude, like the roar of many waters and like the sound of mighty peals of thunder, crying out,
> "Hallelujah!
> For the Lord our God
>   the Almighty reigns.
> Let us rejoice and exult
>   and give him the glory,
> for the marriage of the Lamb has come,
>   and his Bride has made herself ready;
> it was granted her to clothe herself
>   with fine linen, bright and pure"—
> for the fine linen is the righteous deeds of the saints.
>   And the angel said to me, "Write this: Blessed are those who are invited to the marriage supper of the Lamb." (Revelation 19:6–9)

Who is on the invitation list? We all are. All the visions in the book of Revelation leave us with the same question: Whose side are we on? In fact, our choice is not whether to attend the wedding, but whether to marry the Lamb as his bride. The Lamb, of course, is Jesus. As he and his people pledge themselves to each other, all creation joins the celebration.

At the outset of this chapter I promised pictures of two attractive woman. The girl whom Mom won't like, of course, is the whore of Babylon. The lovely, pure, and innocent girl is the bride of Christ, "'clothed with fine linen, bright and pure', for the fine linen is the righteous deeds of the saints." These "saints" are not especially holy people venerated by the church. They are all the people who have sought to live faithfully for Christ through the oppression of the dragon, the beasts, and the whore.

The invitation and proposal to attend this wedding come a chapter earlier as the whore of Babylon is at the peak of her power. "Then I heard another voice from heaven saying, 'Come out of her, my people, lest you take part in her sins'" (Revelation 18:4).

We have to ask ourselves, What would it mean to "come out of" the whore of Babylon? Should any follower of Jesus participating in the infrastructures of commerce quit? Shall we go off the grid, grow our own food, and live in a log cabin we built by ourselves so we don't have to participate in any part of the whore of Babylon?

Over the years many groups have tried this, from the Essenes of Jesus' time, who settled Qumran and collected the Dead Sea Scrolls, to the old-order Amish who regularly parked their horse and buggy in a parking lot across the street from my house. The problem with this approach is the many ways it makes the mission of Israel and the church impossible. How can we bless all nations when we hide our lives away from the world?

Our obedience to God's mission in the world requires us to be, as Jesus said, "in the world but not of the world." We need to go to the grocery store to buy food, to go the mall for clothes and other things we need. Many of us have some kind of pension plan or savings that are invested in businesses around the world. The whore of Babylon is in our face every day. How can we follow Paul's example and use the resources we have from the empire to proclaim the coming of a better kingdom?

Somehow, we must find ways to disentangle ourselves from the whore while continuing to buy and sell what we and others need. John paints the picture of a beautifully attired bride of Christ. The bright, fine linen she wears to the feast, John tells us, "is the righteous deeds of the saints" (Revelation 19:8).

Jesus painted some word pictures of his own. In one he spoke of God separating sheep from goats.

> Then the King will say to those on his right, "Come, you who are blessed by my Father, inherit the kingdom prepared for you from the foundation of the world. For I

> was hungry and you gave me food, I was thirsty and you
> gave me drink, I was a stranger and you welcomed me, I
> was naked and you clothed me, I was sick and you visited
> me, I was in prison and you came to me."... Truly, I say to
> you, as you did it to one of the least of these my brothers
> and sisters, you did it to me. (Matthew 25:34–40)

If we clothe ourselves with righteous deeds such as these, we remain
the radiant bride of Christ despite the lures of the whore of Babylon.

The whore's message, which she quite often persuades the
beast of government to declare, is that we have a civic duty to buy
and consume her goods. Good citizens are good consumers.

Consider that word for a moment: consume. To consume
something is to use it up. When I consume my lunch, there's usu-
ally not too much left over. We are consuming the world God gave
us at an alarming pace. We are using it up and not putting anything
back. How long might we continue to consume until there is nothing left?

The whore of Babylon takes and takes. The bride of Christ
gives and gives. The bride gives herself to God and to others in
need. The whore is working for profit. The bride is working to
make a positive difference. Profit may be a necessity to continue
making that difference, but the point is the good provided to the
community rather than profit. The whore consumes it all, leaving nothing for anyone else. The bride feeds the poor. The bride
clothes the naked. The whore builds walls to keep the poor and the
foreigner away. The bride builds doors to let them in for the feast.
The whore uses people and loves things. The bride loves people
and uses things.

We participate in the commerce of our world either as the
bride or the whore. Mind you, sometimes we can be a bit of both.
But by dressing ourselves in righteous deeds of love and generosity
we are able to move out of the whore of Babylon.

Perhaps we need to develop some spiritual disciplines around
how we spend money and the things we choose to buy. The
whore tells us that we need a myriad of things we don't need. Her

messaging is so strong and prevalent it is hard to even notice her attitude creeping into our own sensibility.

What if we decided to fast from trends for a month, or a year? Trends are one of the very successful ways the whore keeps us consuming things we don't need for her profit. What will be the new color this fall? My clothes are in pretty good shape, but they are last year's color and style! We could defy that trend. We could fast from this year's style.

My phone, my tablet, my television . . . There is always some new piece of technology that makes last year's model completely obsolete! I need more memory! And I need it faster! What if we defied that trend? What if we realized we were quite excited about our phone until they added a higher-resolution camera to the new one, and we could still be just as happy with what we already had? What if we decided to hang on to our technological devices until they literally stopped working? We could fast from the rat race of technology.

We should note that the church itself is not immune from this preoccupation with trends. Perhaps before we launch the next big thing that will make us more effective, we could consider how well we are doing with the big things we have already taken on. Did they enter our DNA, or were they a passing momentarily interest? Are we building long-term relationships for ministry, or so busy turning from one project to another that people are too busy to simply share life together?

What if we took the money we saved through our trend-fast and gave it to support an existing food bank or drop-in for street youth?

The whore of Babylon only has as much control over us as we give her. Simply by conducting our business responsibly for the public good we can break her hold, present the world with an alternative lifestyle, demonstrate to the world that God loves people, and be a radiant bride of Christ, clothed in fine linen.

9

A Living Hope

God hates visionary dreaming; it makes the dreamer proud and preten-
tious. The man who fashions a visionary ideal of community demands
that it be realized by God, by others, and by himself. He enters the
community of Christians with his demands, sets up his own laws, and
judges that brethren and God himself accordingly. He stands adamant,
a living reproach to all others in the circle of brethren. He acts as if he
is the creator of the Christian community, as if his dream binds men
together. When things do not go his way, he calls the effort a failure.
When his ideal picture is destroyed, he sees the community going to
smash. So he becomes, first an accuser of his brethren, then an accuser
of God, and finally the despairing accuser of himself.

—DIETRICH BONHOEFFER, *LIFE TOGETHER*

I WAS JUST BEGINNING ministry in a hurt, exhausted, and disheart-
ened congregation. I was following a very gifted pastor who had
come to the end of his ministry in that church upon the discovery
of moral failure. Before I had learned the layout of the building
people were asking, "What is your vision for us?"

I made a serious mistake no visionary pastor wants to make. I read a great book, *Life Together*, by Dietrich Bonhoeffer.[1] Not even thirty pages in I came to the paragraph quoted above. I recognized my career as pastor in Bonhoeffer's description. Articulate an ideal. Cast a vision. Make less than ideal progress. Become angry at the church for making the poor decision to ignore my leadership; become angry at God for not blessing what I had so clearly designed to glorify him; and become angry with myself for being such a failure at building something beautiful for God.

No wonder so many pastors are tired and burned out! And equally, no wonder so many churches are so exhausted, running from one idea to another, wishing they had a pastor who would simply love God and love them and let God take them wherever he might please.

I suspect this is countercultural for many readers. It is certainly countercultural to empire strategies for church growth and advancement. I am not against the spread of the gospel and finding more effective ways to go about the work of spreading it. My caveat, however, is that our living and proclaiming the gospel needs to be conducted in harmony with the gospel itself. God gives. God gives a Son. God gives a sacrifice. God gives his Spirit. God gives a church. God gives a kingdom.

I grew up in a church that weekly proclaimed "the mystery of faith: Christ died, Christ rose, Christ is coming again!" I believe this sequence of events to be the turning point of all human history. Nothing was the same after these happened.

But the world seems to go on its usual exhausting and exhausted way. I am obviously writing this prior to the time you find yourself reading it. But I suspect that when you read these words today's news still will report wars and rumors of war. There will be earthquakes, hurricanes, flood, and famine. People will continue to turn their backs on the poor. Refugees will be collecting in overnight tent cities but will not find an easy welcome into countries where wealth and opportunity abound. Most sad of all, many Christians remain more part of the problem than the solution.

---

1. Bonhoeffer, *Life Together*.

The weakness of our vision is a product of the weakness of our imagination. I have worked as a professional artist for a number of years. Most of what I have sold are iconic Canadian landscapes. Sometimes I try my hand at abstract art. I admire Jackson Pollock's swirls and Mark Rothko's blocks of simple, deep color, so subtly layered you feel like you could fall into it. People who don't paint look at these works and say, "A child could do it." This is true only in the way a thousand monkeys tapping at typewriters for an infinite amount of time might crank out the complete works of Shakespeare.

By far, the greatest difficulty painting abstractly is a total absence of anything to copy. I can look at a tree and copy it easily. I have done this so often, I can even imagine a tree and paint it from my imagination. But I am only copying the collection of trees I have seen. To begin laying down shape and color without anything to look at to check it against is extremely difficult. If you take your work seriously and plan to show it to anyone else, it is also quite frightening.

It is not hard to envision something that already is, even adding a touch of color here, an extra shape there. When we see the success of the empire's institutions, it comes naturally to envision the church having similar success utilizing similar tools and ideas. We might add a condition here, a caveat there, but we are still copying something that already exists. The empire always evaluates success by measuring something that can be entered into a spreadsheet. We also tend to want to see and count our successes.

In turn, the weakness of our imagination is more than anything else a weakness in our faith. The author of the New Testament Epistle to the Hebrews described faith as "the assurance of things hoped for, the conviction of things not seen" (Hebrews 11:1).

This definition follows closely on the heels of a dire warning. "If we go on sinning deliberately after receiving the knowledge of the truth, there no longer remains a sacrifice for sins, but a fearful expectation of judgment and a fury of fire" (Hebrews 10:26–27). This, in turn, takes us back to a warning a few chapters earlier in the book.

> It is impossible, in the case of those who have once been
> enlightened, who have tasted the heavenly gift, and have
> shared in the Holy Spirit, and have tasted the goodness
> of the word of God and the powers of the age to come,
> and then have fallen away, to restore them again to re-
> pentance, since they are crucifying once again the Son of
> God to their own harm and holding him up to contempt.
> (Hebrews 6:4–6)

There has been a lot of discussion and speculation about what it
might mean to fall away and recrucify Christ in such a manner.
Most explanations boil down to some form of having accepted the
good news of the kingdom—having begun to live in hope of the
coming age of God's restoration and rule—and then renouncing
that belief and experience.

Perhaps the most common interpretation links to early followers of Jesus whose faith could not endure the constant stress of
persecution and pressure. This would certainly be consistent with
how this writer encourages readers to respond to his warnings.

> Recall the former days when, after you were enlightened,
> you endured a hard struggle with sufferings, sometimes
> being publicly exposed to reproach and affliction, and
> sometimes being partners with those so treated. For you
> had compassion on those in prison, and you joyfully ac-
> cepted the plundering of your property, since you knew
> that you yourselves had a better possession and an abid-
> ing one. (Hebrews 10:32–34)

I'm trying to imagine North American Christians in the heart of
our consumeristic empire joyfully accepting the plunder of our
property!

For the writers of the New Testament, persecution and opposition from civic and religious authorities were the normative experience for followers of Jesus. Perhaps for many, at the time they
began their life of faith the danger of being a Jesus follower living
under the thumb of the empire was an exciting and daring adven-
ture. They were on the ground floor of a new and revolutionary

movement. But after a while, that kind of pressure began to wear them down. It was no longer motivational. It was just frightening.

Living within the empire, I personally find the most wearing threat to my faith is not that I am being worn down by constant danger because I might be known as one who stands against the values of the empire. The greatest threat to my faith has generally been boredom. What difference does it actually make that I follow Jesus?

I know Christian people who feel persecuted. Coworkers and neighbors make fun of their faith. They know they are disliked by many people. Truthfully, I don't like them much, either. Their problem is not that they follow Jesus. Their problem is they have confused following Jesus with being obnoxiously dogmatic and judgmental. The worst danger they face is hurt feelings, which are largely a product of reaping what they have sown.

When did it stop being actually dangerous to be a Christian? When the empire could not defeat the church through persecution and intimidation, it did something even worse. The empire began to welcome us and place our leaders in positions of power.

Once we had been tasting the Holy Spirit and "the powers of the age to come." Through the many years of Christendom, we were given a taste of the powers of this present age. We were given armies and thrones. Then we were given parliaments and presidencies. We were given the ability to legislate, coercing dissidents into the empire "built on Judeo-Christian values."

The citizens who did *not* believe and think like official Christians were imprisoned, tortured, and killed by the empire. This does not taste at all like the coming age of God's rule! In some nations this is still the case for people who violate "Christian ethics." There are significant evangelical movements across historically Christianized nations to restore coercion into a particular conservative set of values. Oddly, almost universally these values are limited to issues of gender, sexuality, and reproduction. A significant exception to this is the right to own a gun so no one can plunder our property.

When given the opportunity, we became the empire because, once given the tools of power, all we knew about how to use them was what we had seen. David and Solomon became Pharaoh. The church became Nero. If you think that is extreme, consider Nazi concentration camps and the burning of black churches by white churchgoers in the American South.

This happened because it is so much easier to copy what we have actually seen than it is to imagine what no one has yet seen. Even with a taste of it, we were unable to imagine what the coming age of God's rule might actually look like. It was easier to mount a cross on top of an empire and call it a church than to lay aside the trappings of wealth and power and be the church.

Such failure of imagination was, in fact, a failure of faith. "Faith is the assurance of things hoped for, the conviction of things not seen."

Perhaps the hardest thing to see is the connection between suffering and imagination. Each year many nations celebrate something similar to what we in Canada call Remembrance Day: a day of bringing to mind those who have died in war. This holiday was never meant to be a glorification of war, but a reminder of how everyone suffers in war. Not only soldiers who return home in flag-draped coffins, but other soldiers who return maimed in body and spirit as well. Add to these the spouses, parents, children, siblings, and friends of the fallen, and there is no one who is not touched by war. We recall this as an incentive to pray and work for peace. The suffering of war demands our imagination to find tools for making peace.

It is very unlikely that white people in North America will be able to imagine what racial equality might look like. We haven't suffered racial apathy and cruelty. We did not have our land stolen from beneath our feet with no legal recourse, nor were our grandparents brought here on slave ships.

Our imagination is not stirred until we can really see a black person gasping, "I can't breathe," with a white cop kneeling on his neck. Or hear one of our broken original inhabitants tearfully recall abuses suffered at a residential school. It has taken far too many such images to get our attention.

This is why Christians should be the first to say, "Black and indigenous lives matter." It is not that we devalue other life, but our hearts are tuned to the groans God is listening to.

When, finally, our attention turns to such suffering, when black people and indigenous people show us their suffering, then, through suffering, we might begin to imagine a world without racism. Their recitations of suffering call us to repentance.

But we must understand what repentance actually is. It is not feeling guilty and experiencing sadness because of something that happened in the past. The word translated "repent" in the New Testament literally means to turn around and start walking in the other direction. Repentance is about the future, not the past. We have substituted feelings of sorrow for the prophetic actions God wants us to take.

The people who wrote the New Testament lived in almost immediate expectation of Christ returning to bring the fullness of God's kingdom to fruition. They longed for this coming.

When the empire stopped mistreating us and started electing us to high office, we lost our ability to look at the empire critically and imagine how different it will be when the Coming One comes and reveals the fullness of the powers of the age to come.

It requires no faith to use the tools of empire. As a guest lecturer in a seminary class, I made an off-the-cuff remark that forty years of pastoral ministry had taught me how to win a church fight. I'm a veteran. This wasn't the topic of my talk, but it was the lesson most of the students wanted to learn. It took nearly fifteen minutes to get back on track from this one off-the-cuff comment.

In answer to their questions, I said they really had two choices. The first was to read and digest an old Chinese book about military strategy, *The Art of War*, by Sun Tzu. They could then take those strategies and apply them to all the places they were experiencing conflict and opposition in the church. My experience has been they would win most of the fights. But they wouldn't feel good about it. This strategy would turn them into despots. Successful despots. But despots, nevertheless.

The second choice they might make would be to read and digest Isaiah 53, the description of God's Suffering Servant.

> Like a lamb taken to be slaughtered
>> and like a sheep being sheared,
>> he took it all in silence.
> Justice miscarried, and he was led off—
>> and did anyone really know what was happening?
> He died without a thought for his own welfare,
>> beaten bloody for the sins of my people.
> They buried him with the wicked,
>> threw him in a grave with a rich man,
> Even though he'd never hurt a soul
>> or said one word that wasn't true.
> Still, it's what God had in mind all along,
>> to crush him with pain.
> The plan was that he give himself as an offering for sin
>> so that he'd see life come from it—life, life, and more life.
>> And God's plan will deeply prosper through him.
> Out of that terrible travail of soul,
>> he'll see that it's worth it and be glad he did it.
> Through what he experienced, my righteous one, my servant,
>> will make many "righteous ones,"
>> as he himself carries the burden of their sins.
> Therefore I'll reward him extravagantly—
>> the best of everything, the highest honors—
> Because he looked death in the face and didn't flinch.
> (Isaiah 53:7–12 MSG)

The execution of Jesus is not merely something for us to believe. It is the model and path his followers are to imitate. We are to walk in his steps. Remember WWJD bracelets? What *would* Jesus do? He would embrace suffering to end the suffering of others. If a pastor really wants to win a church fight, the best way to do so is to love our critics rather than defeating them.

This requires not only more faith, more courage, and more blood than vanquishing our foes; it also requires more imaginative faith. If God's servant can be more gracious and forgiving than anyone else in the conflict, at the end of the day most people who follow Jesus will admire and want to imitate one who is willing to endure crucifixion for the sake of their people. In this way the suffering leader "will make many 'righteous ones'" and "see life come from it."

Imaginative faith accepts suffering, learning from it a little more of what God's rule could look like. Turning in a new direction, imaginative faith begins to act as if the rule of God has already come instead of merely building a religious empire.

The Hebrews author reminds us of a long list of people, beginning with Abram, who have lived by imaginative faith.

> These all died in faith, not having received the things promised, but having seen them and greeted them from afar, and having acknowledged that they were strangers and exiles on the earth. For people who speak thus make it clear that they are seeking a homeland. If they had been thinking of that land from which they had gone out, they would have had opportunity to return. But as it is, they desire a better country, that is, a heavenly one. Therefore God is not ashamed to be called their God, for he has prepared for them a city. (Hebrews 11:13–16)

Abram left the Chaldean empire to go to a place of promise without knowing where that place would be. His vision was simple. He would take one step closer to God, and when he had taken that step, take another step closer to God. It was not Abram's vision to build something for God. His vision was to find what God was giving to him. Finding it, he and his children would fill that place in a way that would bless all nations and people on earth. He was looking forward to a future "whose designer and builder is God."

When I had to frame a vision for the members of the hurting congregation described at the start of this chapter, my answer became, "Let's take our vision from Abram. Let's do today what brings us closer to God and his purpose in us and in the city around us, and tomorrow we'll take the next step God offers to us." There was no way to put a big thermometer at the front of the church to measure how we were doing against that goal. Some members would have felt more secure with a thermometer. Others were willing to take a risk in faith believing that God could probably design something for us that would be better than whatever we might design for ourselves.

I don't understand the vision of a heavenly country to be pie in the sky when we finally die. This vision is to be an outpost of heaven on earth. "They acknowledged that they were strangers and exiles on the earth . . . But as it is, they desire a better country, that is, a heavenly one."

Rome was conquering colonies to rob their wealth for the sake of Rome. The church, the community of people who love and follow Jesus, do the opposite. We create colonies of heaven who live as foreigners in this world for the sake of this world.

We look carefully at suffering. We look at our own suffering, which has much to teach us. We look even more closely at the suffering of people different from us, not because they are more important but because their difference makes it harder for us to see them truly. And we ask, If God were to heal what is wounded and broken, what would he do?

When I began to follow Jesus in the 1970s, the evangelical community had a fascination with the idea of Jesus coming again. At least as I was exposed to it, it was a theology of rescue and escape. Jesus would come and snatch the people who loved him from the suffering of this evil world. A corollary of this rescue meant everyone who did not believe in Jesus—and believe in the proper way—would be left behind to endure a time of even more intense suffering.

I suggest that such a theology most likely would arise in the experience of a failing Christian empire. This is why as Christians begin to lose power over culture, many become upset when store clerks wish them a "Happy Holiday" rather than "Merry Christmas." Relatively minor cultural changes feel like major losses.

Thankfully, the understanding of Christ's coming many evangelical Christians have developed in more recent years is somewhat more sophisticated and biblical. The technical word for a theology of the end is *eschatology*.

Healthy eschatology is essential for Christians living in the heart of the empire. It is only through an active eschatology that we can begin to imagine and enact a different way of sharing life together as a human community.

Recently on social media I asked the question, "What would utopia look like for you?" I was hoping to stimulate conversation around ideals and what we can try to move toward. I was surprised and dismayed by some faithful Christians who considered this a useless and irrelevant question. They argued there could be no utopia until Christ comes again, and, at that point, it would be out of our hands. There is some truth in that. But also some evasion. Eschatology was being used as a way to evade the responsibility of trying to live as an outpost of heaven on earth.

This evasion is easy and safe. It allows us to enjoy the benefits of the present empire in which we find ourselves without needing to have concern for people outside the empire who live in oppression and poverty. Additionally, such an evasion allows us to avoid critiquing our empire and attracting the ire of the powerful.

But it completely fails the Christian mission to be God's people in the world: to live as foreigners in order to be a blessing to all nations and peoples.

Eschatology is meant to provide us with a vision of the next step we can take to demonstrate and articulate what the rule of God looks like. Learning from the suffering empires have generated, we can begin to formulate a community that is organized around different principles.

This community will reverse the effects of the Tower of Babel as it rejects the division of human persons between us and them. People of every tribe, tongue, nation will have a place in this community because we are one in Christ.

Like Moses imagining the un-empire the tribes of Israel were meant to become, this community will begin to organize itself to share wealth and resources more equitably. The stranger and refugee will be as welcome at the dinner table as any other member of the family. We remember that we, too, were once slaves, but, hearing us groan, God came to set us free.

This community is seeking God, knowing that God is free. He does not live in temples made with human hands, nor is he under the control of political, social, or even religious leaders. He is for the poor, the marginalized, the wounded. We often hear his voice through our sons and daughters, our servants, and our elderly.

This community is not afraid to suffer because it knows that a seed only bears fruit after it has fallen to the earth and died. This community is the body of Christ on earth.

Our world does not need more Christians in power. Our world needs more Christians with imagination and faith who are daily praying, "Your will be done on earth as it is in heaven."

Bibliography

Bonhoeffer, Dietrich. *Life Together*. New York: HarperOne, 2009.

Brueggemann, Walter. *Prophetic Imagination*. Philadelphia: Fortress, 1978.

Ehrenberg, V., and A. H. M. Jones. *Documents Illustrating the Reigns of Augustus and Tiberius*. 2nd ed. Oxford: Clarendon, 1955.

Sider, Ronald J. *Rich Christians in an Age of Hunger*. Downers Grove: InterVarsity, 1977.

www.ingramcontent.com/pod-product-compliance
Lightning Source LLC
Chambersburg PA
CBHW071053090426
42737CB00013B/2342